Psychology of Everyday Life

100 Essays on the Psychology of Our Everyday
Issues

Daniel Grandinettti
Translated by Sabrina de Paula

TABLE OF CONTENTS

This book is dedicated to the general public. It addresses Psychological issues of interest to our daily lives in the form of short essays, in a language that is accessible to lay people, although not trivial. In this preface, however, I ask permission to address my fellow psychologists. Other readers can certainly follow what I will say, because although I speak to professional psychologists, the issue is also interesting for most.

Psychology has been seeking its true object since its alleged foundation as science, in 1879. Several lines and methodologies have emerged over time in order to provide it with an objective approach on the mind and behavior. Approaches that were more subjective and more distant from an ideal scientific psychology also proliferated. There has always been much discussion about the actual scientific achievements of the objective approaches and about the shortcomings that kept subjective approaches away from science. Many agreed and still agree to say that the greatness, the development, and the effective establishment of theoretical and practical Psychology depend on its implementation as science. However, in my view, Psychology's incipient state and its constant inability to establish itself in the theoretical, practical, and social fields has nothing to do with the lack of scientificity. A psychology widely recognized for its scientific status by both the academic community and by public opinion, would not necessarily fulfill Psychology's ideals of greatness. What prevents Psychology from fulfilling its greatness is not the absence of scientificity. On the contrary, the blind pursuit of scientificity has been a cause of difficulty that Psychology has always faced in the search for its true object.

For Psychology, the pursuit of scientificity has always walked hand in hand with medicalization. And when I say medicalization, I'm not saying that Psychology seeks or has sought to become a therapy that uses drugs, which would be, I think, absurd. But although the development of psychological therapy has kept itself away from drugs, it has always sought medicalization.

Disease is the object of Medicine. Diseases are whatever is out of the norm established by Medicine itself. The standard, for Medicine, is health. I think there is no doubt that most people are healthy and live healthy most of the time. Disease is the exception in the life of most people. Therefore, Medicine deals with the exceptions to the rule. Its goal is to develop therapies that are more effective against diseases. Moreover, since diseases are exceptions to the rule, the purpose of Medicine is to develop therapeutics that are useful to the small portion of society affected by them. However, disease is not part of the life of those infected only; it is part of everyone's life, because we can all get sick at any moment. In addition, the reality of disease is hard. Becoming ill is neither easy on the patient nor on their loved ones. All this makes Medicine essential to society, even for those who rarely need it during their lifetime.

Medicine would never be so important if it had not become effective in its proposal. Over time, it has always advanced a little further and achieved success in treatments for diseases that had no solution for many centuries. Consequently, medical knowledge has also come a long way. The understanding acquired by Medicine on the causes of disease progressed at the same rate in which the therapies effectiveness advanced. Today, Medicine is a discipline of widely recognized practical and theoretical status.

Psychology has always lived in the shadow of Medicine. I say this not so much because public opinion has always compared the results of psychological and medical therapies, with possible discrediting of Psychology. I say this, in fact, because the very psychologists have taken the practical and theoretical model of Medicine and applied it to Psychology. As the object of Medicine is the exception to the rule, psychologists of many different lines and approaches also turned their attention primarily to what is not normal. Psychology has always been concerned with psychic disorders, neuroses and psychoses. And this is by no means an exclusive feature of the objective and scientistic lines. The more subjective approaches also theorize primarily on disorders and mental illnesses. So even though not openly defending the

10

medicalization of Psychology, it is the psychologists themselves who strive to make it ever more like a medical specialty.

Psychology is not and cannot be a medical specialty. Consequently, it was inevitable for Psychology to be marked by a strong contradiction in its effort to medicalize itself. Although theoretical Psychology deals with disorders and diseases, the psychologist practice essentially deals with normality. Clinical psychologists represent the majority of Psychology professionals and, in his office, the clinical psychologist deals with the most common issues of everyday life. However, the same psychologist whose practice is guided by normality deals with mental disorders or diseases is in his theoretical research. The psychologist who is daily confronted by life's most mundane questions and is required to find increasingly effective solutions for them is the same who dreams of developing revolutionary therapies for diseases that attack a tiny portion of the population. A given psychologist, for example, receives in his office a boy who exchanged glances with a girl sitting at the next table in the bar. This boy seeks the Psychology professional because he did not know how to react or deal with the anxiety caused by the situation. The psychologist intervenes, helps him with his problem, and soon after returns to his research in the field of autism and schizophrenia.

In Medicine, theory relates to practice. A doctor researches on what he works with. In Psychology, there is a gap between theory and practice. The psychologist does not research about the subject of his work – or at least, does not research on the most recurring subjects. Consequently, there are no books of Psychology dealing with life's everyday issues. Theoretical books of Psychology are either written about abnormality or methodology. The anguish that so frequently invades our everyday lives finds no room in psychological literature. Hence, it is not at all surprising the fact that self-help literature proliferates so much. It proliferates because it finds no competition! Self-help books dominate alone and undisturbed the market segment that deals with life's everyday difficulties.

Psychology's practical object is ordinary life. Its theoretical object, however, has been whatever is extraordinary. Society has

11

always expected Psychology would provide aid to everyday problems. But psychologists, intoxicated by the dream of sharing Medicine's same magnitude, dedicated themselves to finding answers to the rule exceptions. Proof that society has always expected Psychology to constitute knowledge about the everyday problems is the fact that psychologists were called to talk about this subject in the media. And the annoying triviality with which they respond to this demand shows that, in fact, Psychology does not have an established knowledge about it.

Society has already understood that the object of Psychology is everyday life and its problems. Psychologists are yet to understand it. Psychologists are yet to understand that Psychology's knowledge must be compatible with its clinical practice. They are yet to understand that the knowledge produced by Psychology must feed on clinical practice and that clinical practice, in turn, must develop itself with the help of guidelines indicated by that knowledge. What preserves Psychology in its smallness is the refusal to embrace its proper object. What preserves the smallness of Psychology is the endless race for a greatness that was never its own. The psychologist dreams of doing science and developing revolutionary approaches to disorders and diseases because that was how Medicine achieved its greatness. Deluded by the belief that this should also be the ideal of greatness for Psychology, he glances at the trivialities of everyday life with disdain. What interests the psychologist in clinical practice is not so much the everyday life that comes through his office door. What interests the psychologist in clinical practice is the possibility to diagnose, predict, make interventions and "cure" patients. In short, the psychologists are interested in this "play doctor" which they call "clinical practice".

The object of Psychology is everyday life and its problems. The magnitude of Psychology depends on theoretical Psychology focusing its efforts on our daily lives. Up to now, no discipline produced knowledge about everyday problems. None of them managed to do that because that is Psychology's task; task which has been refused so far. For having chased a greatness that was never its own, Psychology has left untouched the possibility of becoming great. And if the greatness of Psychology depends on establishing knowledge about everyday life, the scientificity issue is a secondary one. The question "is it or is it not possible to build scientific knowledge about everyday life" is less important than the need to have Psychology build this knowledge, be it scientific or not. If scientific grounding is impossible for an everyday psychology, then we must base it in different grounds, and we must do it as well as we can without the aid of science.

The fundamental theme of everyday life is our daily anguish, the difficulties of our relationships and our pursuit of happiness. In short, the fundamental theme of the psychology of everyday life is our struggle with the lack of meaning and our quest for it, from the most simple and trivial things to the most universal issues which mobilize us the most. Therefore, we must take great care so that the attempt to bring this psychology into science does not change its essence. If scientifization of Psychology can only occur at the cost of losing its existential value, science should be left aside. And I talk about existential value because any psychology that dedicates itself to everyday life inevitably becomes existentialist. How can we talk about everyday things, the numerous issues that disturb us and cross our path, without analyzing their meaning and the value they add to life? If the object of Psychology is everyday life, and if all psychologies of everyday life become existential, then the theoretical maturity of Psychology is in existentialism. I am not saying that all psychologies should be excluded in favor of the current forms of existentialism, and I am not claiming that existentialism is in any advantage in relation to other theoretical lines. I am saying that any psychology that theoretically deals with our day-to-day will eventually become existential in its own way, not necessarily the way of current existentialism which, by the way, falls short a number of times for focusing on death and major existential questions instead of dealing with everyday trivia. Existentialism, when focused on day-to-day, discovers the anguish of life is caused by life itself, not by death.

Psychology's main object is our everyday life. It is to this object that Psychology devotes its practice; in theory, it should be

13

Psychology's main concern. The debates surrounding disease and mental disorders and the psychologists' involvement in social affairs and the anti-asylum fight, for example, are very important. I do not intend to deny the importance of that. I merely wish to point out that none of this is Psychology's main object. It's not about discussing whether the world's serious social issues are more important than common questions in everyday life. It's about recognizing that, regardless of how important each question is on its own, Psychology's object is everyday life. Here in Brazil, besides striving for medicalization, Psychology continually strives to prove its social importance. The way the Psychology council system is administered implies the fear that if Psychology does not prove its social value every day, it will end up with no arguments to prove its general value. However, the sense of "social value" that drives this effort is quite restricted. By "social value" we understand Psychology's effective involvement in working with the poorest classes. The "social value" is extracted, thus, from Psychology's actual results in issues that are more or less specific of such classes. However, intervention in everyday life issues has considerable social value. The anguish of our day-to-day is a problem that does not choose classes. Both the employer and the employee are required to deal with it, each in their own way. Knowing everyday life's problems and anguish is critical for any social work directed to the poorer classes, especially in order to avoid the common mistake to reduce all human suffering to material issues.

The object of this book is everyday life; Psychology applied to everyday life. It is practical Psychology expressed in words; practical Psychology which has never been given the right to present itself as "Psychology", has never been registered, formulated and is still imprisoned within four walls. Practical Psychology, the psychology expressed only behind closed doors, needs to speak up! We need to give the floor to practical Psychology since it is through practical Psychology that psychologists and patients find the meaning of everyday life. The function of Psychology is to find the words to express this meaning. The function of Psychology is to draw attention to everything that goes unnoticed in us day-to-day, and that takes

14

control of the situation in an unnoticed way. This is practical Psychology. This is everyday Psychology and its purpose. This will be the purpose, I hope, of all psychologies from now on.

The Author
Belo Horizonte, May 2015

When we seek someone to talk to about our problems sometimes that person, after listening to some of what we have to say, starts explaining how everything was the result of our own mistakes and how "if we hadn't done this or that, such a thing wouldn't have happened", etc. This strategy rarely proves itself productive. Generally, it only serves to further increase the anguish of those seeking help. Those who look for someone to talk to basically expect two things: (1) that the person he sought will point out concrete and realistic solutions and (2) that the person understands the drama being narrated, demonstrating empathy and solidarity. As option (1) is often unavailable, only option (2) remains. In fact, even when (1) is available, (2) remains crucial. People who need to talk are suffering from loneliness and need to share their anguish with someone in order not to feel so lonely. So when they receive in response an "analysis" of how everything is "their own fault" before there has been any manifestation of empathy or sympathy, the message acquires the following meaning: "You have no reason to be suffering; after all, you have yourself to blame for it all. Therefore, I deny you my sympathy."

Being "guilty" or not when going through a problem does not diminish one's suffering. Regardless of whose "guilt" it is, the problem is there and the suffering is real. Pointing the finger at the person and saying he is to blame for it all solves nothing. Quite the contrary. Denying solidarity, you will make the person even more distressed and helpless, as he will be forced to carry alone the burden of certain attitudes that at that moment, he doesn't really understand and doesn't know how to change.

So why do people give this kind of response? Some intuitively feel that if a problem is happening to others, it could also happen to them. Therefore, it is comforting to imagine that someone else is going through a hard time because he made many dumb mistakes, for this enables the conclusion that "if such things have never happened to me, it means I have not made the same mistakes. And because I do not make the same mistakes, I will

17

most likely not have to go through this chagrin". Blaming others for their own problems helps creating the illusion that fate is in our hands (as well as that person's fate is in their own hands), that "will is power" and that we will only go through hard times if we want and deserve to.

002 – WHY DO WE FEEL WE NEED TO HUMILIATE PEOPLE?

Our personality is formed through our identification with others. So when we learn to speak the language of a community and incorporate the values, customs and opinions of the people around us, we are building our own identity. This is a huge paradox and a great contradiction, because the more identical we become to the world and others, the more aware of our individuality we are. No wonder we use the expression "identity" to refer to the individuality that defines us. We use the term "identity" because individuality is built as we establish an identity with the world. A well-structured personality has a rock solid identification with the world.

Our individuality is a paradox because our relationship with the people we identify with is paradoxical. While we make them our identity, we also make them the denial of that identity. It is the fact that we identify with them that makes us aware of the difference between them and ourselves. If by identifying with others we become aware of the difference between them and ourselves, they represent the identity that we still haven't realized with our Self. In other words, the others represent what we want to be but we are not yet. As such, they are the denial of our identity, or the awareness that we aren't what we want to be.

To the extent that we realize our identity in relation to people, this relationship is marked by a variety of loving and positive feelings. But to the extent that we find the denial of our identity within them, the result is the feeling of inferiority and the feelings based on it, such as jealousy, envy, anger, etc. Both completion and negation are present in every relationship, although one of them can be more conscious. Thus, even in the most affectionate and loving relationships there is a feeling of inferiority that makes us feel sometimes alone, abandoned, ignored by the person we love so much. And when we feel inferior, our natural reaction is to try to make the other person feel even more inferior in relation to us than we felt in relation to them at that moment. We respond with contempt in words and deeds, with destructive criticism, irony, and sarcasm that make little of what they are and what they do. Such behavior constitutes the vain effort to feel superior in relation to those we consider superior to us, and to make them feel as inferior in relation to us as we feel in relation to them. Even in the most positive and fraternal relationships we find moments like these, which can be subtle enough to go unnoticed. However, even if they are evident, they can become so common that their real motivation – the feeling of inferiority – gets completely lost in unconsciousness, leaving only the proud conviction that we really consider others inferior to us.

003 – WHY CAN'T WE STOP THINKING ABOUT OUR FEARS?

When Freud proposed the "death drive" concept, many questioned it, including psychoanalysts. Do we all have an unconscious desire to die? In fact, the "death drive" is a very simple – and true – idea. The desire to live and to be accomplished in life encounters many obstacles in life itself. Life frustrations prevent the life within us to be fulfilled. The desire to live, then, contradicts itself: if life is an obstacle to life itself, then we must end life so that it can be fulfilled. The death drive is nothing but a type of life drive, and vice versa. After all, why would someone want to die if not to end all suffering and bring down the obstacles that stop the realization of the desire to live?

If on one hand death drive is a type of life drive, on the other hand it conflicts with the desire to live. If life obstacles make life difficult, death makes life simply impossible. The contradiction between life drive and death drive brings the wish to die into consciousness as the fear of death. The desire to die is a threat to the desire to live; and since the desire to live is preponderant, the desire to die emerges into consciousness as the fear to die. No wonder people who are most extroverted and full of life are also those who most commonly think of death and are afraid of it.

The same applies to other fears. The fear of being betrayed by a love partner is a good example. The loneliness and helplessness that are always present even in the most perfect romantic relationships make the relationship become an obstacle to itself – or an obstacle to the fulfillment of that ideal and perfect relationship everyone wants, but doesn't actually exist. And when the consequent contradictory desire to end the relationship so that it is fulfilled is not properly recognized as such, it ends up being projected onto the partner as his desire to betray us and end it all. The fear, in this case, can be so great and it can become so real that the jealous partner ends up cheating on the other partner before he can do the same. The desire to be in a relationship, in contradiction with itself, ends the relationship that should fulfill it.

The fact that we deeply desire that which we fear can be truly disturbing. In some cases, this fact is evident. Most people can be fully sure that their fear of heights is due to the overwhelming desire to throw themselves at free fall. This fear is a consequence of the struggle against the urge to jump and also a consequence of the conflict between the urge to jump and the desire to stay on dry land. Others can also be clearly aware that their fear of public speaking and exposure is at least proportional to the desire to speak and show off. But what can we say about the fear of getting physically and emotionally hurt, or the fear of failure? What about the fear of seeing our greatest dreams crumble, or the fear of losing the people we love the most? In such cases, things are not easy. The hardest is to answer the question: Why would I be able to want all this? Finding the answer often requires a great analytical effort and the assistance of a psychologist.

The greater the fear and the desire not to think of it, the stronger it appears in thought. Because the greater the fear, the greater the unconscious desire for it to happen, and an unfulfilled desire never leaves us alone.

Being close to a depressed person bothers many people. People do not know how to react to someone's plea in this state. The cause of this nuisance is quite simple: Depressed people dare doubt that life has meaning, and with that they undermine the strenuous effort that others do to keep their optimism and enthusiasm for life alive. The depressed don't have to say anything to cause this impact. Their mere presence serves to expose the artificiality that underlies our joy in living. For this reason, no one takes depressed people seriously. Overall, people try to (1) encourage them, as one shakes a rattle to a crying child; (2) flood them with advice that are full of clichés, as if depression was a state of mental weakness; or else (3) severely reprove their attitude, as if being depressed was a moral transgression.

The very condition of being depressed poses a serious question about the meaning of life which depressed people themselves are often unable to understand. A large number of people cannot say why they are depressed. And the attitude of those surrounding them tends to reinforce this alienation. People alienate the depressed of their condition so that they themselves do not have to face the challenge brought by the depressed. The depressed are treated like children who need to be cheered up, idiots who know nothing of life or transgressors of life itself. And when none of this works, they are finally treated as sick people. The depressed are sent to psychiatrists so that awareness of their questions about life can be definitely numbed.

The meaning of life is manufactured by us. Depression exposes this farce. It exposes the fact that we manufacture the meaning of life with our plans, dreams, projects, hopes; that is, it exposes the fact that we fabricate the meaning of life with speculation about what we haven't done, what we don't have yet, what we can't yet be. The material used to manufacture the meaning of life is emptiness. The depressed dare recognize that emptiness within themselves, and in doing so they insult the dogmatism of those who strive fervently to believe that the emptiness is filled.

Depressed people don't want anyone to try to cheer them up, to give them advice or moral exhortations. The depressed want to be taken seriously. They want to find in somebody else the same question they are asking. They want their emptiness to be understood and accepted naturally. In short, they want to be listened to. Simply listened to. And they discover that it is virtually impossible. It is virtually impossible for anyone to listen to depressed people without trying to cheer them up, without giving them advice, without issuing moral exhortations or without telling them to see a psychiatrist.

Depressed people discover that the fate of the emptiness they had the gall to even realize is isolation and loneliness. They feel that if this gap were fully understood and freely shared by all, maybe it could acquire a sense; a sense that is situated in the present, not the sense manufactured with a future that does not exist. However, since depressed people live in a world that is terrified of the truth they bring and a world which does everything not to take them seriously, they end up not taking themselves seriously and not understanding that which they, after all, are questioning. By result, we have depression treated as an illness and depressed people who, accepting their ill condition, seek medical treatment without having the slightest idea that they bring within themselves healing seeds to a world that insists in living ill by excessive optimism and happiness.

005 – WHY IS IT SO HARD TO FEEL FREE?

All children confronted with limits and prohibitions imposed by their parents dream of growing up so they are able to do anything they want, as if adulthood represented total freedom. Most teens, when faced with a world dominated by restrictions, laws, and social rules, dream of an alternative society where "Do what thou wilt shall be the whole of the law", as if a law-free society were free. Adults feed dreams and career ambitions that have only the sky for a limit, as if they could become completely free in the limitless world conquest, and their value as individuals could be fulfilled without limitations.

Personal fulfillment is not related to the absence of limits. Life without limits is not free, it's just unsupported. Limits bolster us. When we receive a hug, the limits imposed on us by the other person's body are the limits of our own bodies. In the awareness of the limitations imposed by someone else, we realize the full and warm awareness of ourselves. A person who never receives a hug never experiences the restrictions of another body against his own body, and therefore remains helpless. However, the same restrictions that define us also state our ambitions: expanding, transcending, overcoming all limits, indefinitely. The warm body of another who embraces us is the limit we want to transcend. But all efforts to wrap them in our arms are useless. The limits never give in, even though the experience of trying to overcome them is pleasant and worthy of our most sincere surrender.

A child suffering many restrictions dreams of living without them; the child who suffers no restriction at all is all tantrums to provoke it. Limits define not only who we are but also what we want to be. So, transcending them doesn't mean eliminating them, but repositioning and restructuring them. It's foolish to believe in freedom as the absence of limits. It's foolish to believe limits are a hindrance to freedom. A free individual is one who won't be imprisoned, but also won't do without limits. Freedom is the ability to be flexible with one's own limitations; to respect them and defend them when necessary, to overcome them when possible; never to overthrow them or eliminate them.

One who sees limits as barriers to freedom and who dreams of a limitless freedom will never feel free, for even if it were possible to live in a world without barriers, the simple lack of restrictions would represent the greatest of all limitations. After all, the will aims to go beyond its limits – whatever they may be. And the will which finds no limits to transcend is prevented from acting; it is the will limited to the extreme.

Those who preserve a teenager attitude throughout life, who interpret all forms of restriction as an affront to freedom, those who proclaim life without limits as the only way of living possible

23

and who follow the premise of "Banning is banned" actually love the restrictions which restrain them. They love the limits they criticize so strongly, they worship the prohibitions they so fiercely condemn. For these people, the absolute realization of the will is in outrage, in transgression, and revolt. A world in which there were nothing to affront, nothing to transgress, nothing to rebel against would be meaningless. It is only in outrage, in transgression, and revolt that these people feel absolute freedom. The more authoritarian and prohibitive the world in which they live is, the more rejoicing will be their sense of freedom.

We only feel free when we are limited by the world around us. To be free is to be aware of one's own limits. Freedom exists only within certain limitations. But this is not easy to understand, for people generally tend to oppose the notion of "freedom" to the notion of "limit". And those who can't harmonize the two notions will only feel totally free if harder limits are imposed on them, and vice versa.

006 – THE WORST LONELINESS LIES IN THE FEELING OF INFERIORITY

Social networks only imitate life. People are concerned about presenting their contacts with images of a life full of success, optimism, lovers and friends in social networks as well as in real life. Who among us has never felt his life was tremendously dull after entering a social network and seeing so many pictures of couples in love and a bunch of close friends enjoying nightlife? There are so many smiles... so much joy! The same thing happens in real life. People around us are always smiling, they are always happy. We even envy their problems because they face them with such optimism and confidence in the future that we come to ask, "Gee, it must be so nice to trust that the future will be wonderful! Why can't I be sure about mine?"

Living around such perfect people is not easy. Where is all that which doesn't fit this perfection, because it is all so human? It stays buried deep inside the soul and hidden away from everything and everyone. In my experience as a psychologist, most clients come to the office with a negative image of themselves. They often seek a psychologist for thinking they're crazy or something alike. So once they feel a little safer, they confess the awkwardness with their insecurities, ideas, and desires. All they think, desire, or fear is very common, it's all absolutely human. However, they bring the firm conviction of being the only ones who think or feel that way. They feel different from everyone else, different for the worse, and so they start thinking they're crazy or that no one else goes through the same problems. It doesn't even cross their minds that people around them who try so hard to convey the image of perfection also have the same thoughts and the same feelings... but are doing everything to hide it.

It's ironic that, outside the office, these same clients also strive to convey the image of a perfect life in which they don't think and don't feel what they just recently confessed to their psychologist. These clients are also part of the problem. And it doesn't even cross their minds that the loneliness experienced by them in living with people committed to looking perfect is also felt by those same people in their company.

If our "all too human" side were shared, the feeling of inferiority – originated from the illusion of being the only imperfect creature in a world of gods – and the consequent loneliness that accompanies this feeling would not exist. The worst loneliness lies in the illusion of being alone in imperfection. The much acclaimed joy of the Brazilian people, who never lose their smile in the midst of so many difficulties is perfectly understandable. People who share the same environment and the same difficulties feel the weight of problems much lighter. If everyone around us is unemployed, we will suffer much less because of the responsibility of getting a job and the anguish of being unemployed. We will most likely meet with friends going through the same problem so that, at a local bar, we can sing a song and laugh about it. But if we live in an environment where everyone else is employed and thriving, the burden of the responsibility and the anxiety will be greater and we will rarely joke about it.

The sharing of our "all too human" side is what makes us equal to all people. And there is only peace of mind when we identify with those around us.

007 – THE HEAVY BURDEN OF "WILL IS POWER"

One of the strongest and most current philosophies of our time is summed up in a single short sentence: "will is power". This sentence is always used to promote extra-strong doses of motivation, commitment, and willpower for those facing difficulties, who need to overcome an obstacle or reach some objective. By the same token, psychologists who work with HR, do motivational speaking or deal with self-help psychology are always repeating that same philosophy. And the extensive use of that old formula drains the strength of many people.

There is no doubt that the optimistic belief in willpower has led many to great results. It is also quite likely that people are able to always do more for themselves. You can always go a little beyond. My experience in clinical psychology shows that people are able to overcome difficulties which they themselves believed not being able to win, and able to find strength within themselves which they never realized was there. Psychotherapy is a self-analysis process in which we better understand both ourselves and the world around us. In becoming more aware of our fears, desires, the world's real possibilities, we increase o. our ability to act on it to produce the results we expect. However, a person unaware of his fears, who does not know precisely what he wants and does not know enough about the world and its possibilities, may not be fully able to put aside silly fears and go in pursuit of his deepest desires. In such cases, the mere insistence on the old "self-overcoming" and "will is power" formula can lead to exhaustion and to an extreme sense of helplessness and failure. When someone believes to have done everything possible, to have exhausted all strength at his disposal and can no longer see in the world a real possibility, it is cowardice to insist with that person in the "self-overcoming" and "will power to go further" jargons. It is inhumane to confront a person who just failed with the criticism that he only failed because he did not have enough willpower, and that the result would have been different if she had really shown desire to win. The belief that success and failure depend solely on willpower leads us to conclude that our will is null every time we fail even though we are confident of having done the best. "Achieving success is so simple" – we think – "all it takes is willpower. And if my will cannot do something so simple, then I am null as a person and I'm completely powerless." The requirement to put more and more commitment and effort into a goal that we still do not know how to achieve is grueling and exhausting.

In a world ruled by the "will is power" theory, it is believed that the difference between success and failure lies only on willpower. Victorious people win only because they struggle, fight and triumph on their own merit. When people fail, it's because they didn't fight and made no effort; they deserved to fail. The world today is torn between victorious superheroes endowed with super willpower and losers with no willpower at all. But the winners who love to exalt their own merits and enjoy themselves imagining their climb to success as a heroic myth of effort and overcoming forget all the favorable conditions they encountered along the way – and recognizing them may hurt their pride and cause them great pain. Losers who beat their chests and put all the blame on themselves for their luck make the same mistake, and do not consider the unfavorable conditions they that had to face. Self-unawareness is directly proportional to unawareness of the world.

008 – THE MAN OF TODAY IS A "MEGALOMANIAC NOTHING"

In the eternal conflict between theory and practice, the world today overestimates practice. In job interviews, the candidate is required to demonstrate "proactivity", "teamwork skills" and "leadership skills". The job market is looking for professionals with technical courses, those who know better than anyone else "how to" execute a specific function. There is no room for thinking heads. They are too theoretical. In psychology offices, clients arrive wondering "how to" solve their problems. They are not interested in the process of self-knowledge. It's too theoretical. They seek practical responses, preferably simple and quick, because their heads are already busy with a million concerns.

Exaggeration always ends in contradiction, and this case is not different. Thus we see that the most practical people nowadays are also the most theoretical. They have knowledge about practices that exceed their life experience, and so they begin theorizing about "how to do" things or about "how one should do" things which they know nothing of. They are theoretical because their practical knowledge is not experimental, it is theoretical. They issue opinions and advises on any matter that is put into debate, since the people who opine and advise are precisely the ones who know the least. There is a committee and a formed opinion for everything. In Psychology, the urgency of achieving practical results made us enter the era of brief therapies. The client brings a specific problem and the psychologist, in 10 sessions or less, will instruct the client "how to" overcome it. There is no time to lose. And psychologists themselves are the first to overvalue the practice. They reject all theories as "speculative explanatory fictions". The only safe haven is the science that tells us objectively "how to do" things right. The younger and more inexperienced the psychologist, the greater his tendency to believe he can get from books and science the understanding which he couldn't draw on his own from life itself. Science is the new light, "the way and the truth and the life".

Carl Gustav Jung wrote that "People who are only rational have little influence; they are all about the speech, and speech won't take you too far". Knowledge turned into information. Information flows freely; everyone has access to it. Soon, everyone has knowledge about everything, everyone knows "how to do" anything. The most important issues are decided in polls and surveys whose only options are "yes" or "no", "for" or "against". Life itself has become a multiple choice test where the standard answer is the "guess". Everyone knows everything, and nobody is able to change anything. An individual who is full of practical

28

theories already accepts as an absolute truth that nothing can be produced by someone alone. Only teamwork is productive. A single person does not exercise any influence. A single person is now worthless.

Paradoxically, the same people who are worthless and are filled of worthless practical theories are the ones who most strongly cultivate blind faith in willpower and personal power. Today's man is a megalomaniac "nothing". Today's men are as empty of themselves as they are full of faith in their own "personal" power. But what can these men really do for themselves and the world they live in? What can they do but wear their company shirt as a second skin and use their personal power to annul themselves in the pursuit of higher productivity? How far they can go armed only with a bunch of empty practical theories and belief in willpower? What future does this world hold?

009 – WHY ARE WE AFRAID OF CONFRONTATION?

Fear of confrontation... fear of disagreeing with people... fear of complaining of others. What's behind it? At what point did we stop being children who say everything with sincerity to say only what others want to hear?

One who disagrees with others is subject to have others disagree with him as well. One who complains of others is subject to have others complain about him also. In disagreeing or complaining about others, we learn that this behavior increases the chances of having others paying us back disagreeing and complaining about us. It is precisely this "payback" we fear. We are not afraid to disagree or complain about others; we fear that others will disagree or complain about us.

And why do we have this fear?

Small children learn quickly that their lives depend on the assistance of others. If the relationship with others is cut, they will die. At this stage, the dependence between the child and the other is real: it is his physical survival at stake. If the child's existence depends on the other, the other is the base of the child's existence.

29

If the other is the base of the child's existence, the child's existence is within the other. The child is in his own other; soon, the child is the other of himself. The child grows, and the physical dependence with the other ceases to exist. But the child continues to seek the foundation of his "being" on the other. The child's search for himself within the other is called "identification", and the product of the identification between the child and the other is his own Self. The Self is its own other. The Self is the other who, made subjective, became the Self. But the reality of the other made subjective remains dependent on the relationship with the exterior other, real people with whom we interact. Because the exterior other is the real other. The other within, so-called "I", is the internalization of exterior other. Consequently, the existence of the Self depends on identifying with others. If the identification with others is shaken, the Self feels its existence threatened.

When people disagree or complain about us, we interpret this as a breakup, though temporary, of the identificatory relationship with them. The identification with the other is shaken, and with it the very existence of the Self is also shaken, since the identity of the Self is the other. Threats to psychological existence of the Self are meant as real; as real as physical threats. The hopes of a future event that may shake the self-esteem of the Self has the same meaning of waiting for death. Consciously, we know that we won't die and that life will go on, no matter what happens. Still, there is a force or unconscious motivation that makes us wait for the event as if in it there were great chance for us to die. Therefore, shocks to the identity of the Self, such as disagreements or complaints of others, are objects of our fear.

If the identity of the Self is the other, the actions of others are not the only ones that can shake it. Our reactions may also have the same effect. When someone disagrees or complains about us, it's not so much the disagreement or the complaints that frighten us, but all the emotions awaken by the situation. We fear we will feel diminished, abandoned, and lonely. We are especially afraid of our aggressiveness. Aggressive reactions can lead to unpredictable consequences. They can change our relationship with people for the worse and further shake our identity with them. We fear our aggressiveness. We fear the "little devil" that whispers in our ear: "I have to do something, anything, to defend my position. I can't leave it at that! It's this "little devil" who leads us into making the greatest mistakes, and our fear of this little devil is more than justified.

010 – SUFFERING NOT EXPRESSED IN WORDS IS MUFFLED BY DRUGS

People in poor/developing countries suffer miserable material conditions: hunger, disease, homelessness, premature death. Consequently, it's a common practice for these societies to give great importance to material suffering, the suffering that is visible to the eye. This can be observed in the political attitude of students in Brazilian universities: young activist students speak of the elimination of poverty and class distinctions as if that were enough to end suffering in the world. They believe that suffering finds no reason in the absence of material needs. Assigning nonmaterial causalities to that suffering is to treat it with "psychologisms". Only material suffering is real.

In fact, there is another form of suffering that is recognized as real by common sense: suffering for love. The same student who protests in the streets against social inequality publishes romantic verses in the university newsletter. Our society lives in the extremes of materialism and romanticism. If you don't suffer from hunger, disease, death of your loved ones, financial hardship or romantic trouble – or the lack of such trouble – then you have no real reason to suffer. But what about suffering that doesn't fit into any of these categories? I bet many are wondering: "What other reasons may a person have to suffer but material hardship or romantic suffering? Can't all of our problems be reduced to money or love issues?"

Yes, it is possible to reduce all our problems to romantic or material issues. Freud reduced the causes of all our problems to the self-preservation drive and the sexual instinct, later acknowledging that the self-preservation instinct was also sexual.

31

Freud was a man ahead of his time, and he left us a theory that still hasn't been well understood. But he was also a man of his own time, and we can see this in his theory. If on one hand the reduction of all problems to romantic and material issues expands our consciousness, on the other hand it limits the meaning which can be given to suffering. If suffering doesn't find precise meaning in the right words it is experienced as anguish, and anguish is the access road to both anxiety and depression.

People can't tell why they suffer. They get depressed without knowing why; they suffer anxiety attacks for no conscious reason. Many lead a seemingly perfect life. They have the best of everything, they are beautiful, they are in loving relationships, yet they are depressed or anxious. Many of them are full of explanations that refer to the past, to their first affective relationships with others and the world. But they're not able to find the right words to express the deep meaning their pain has for them now! They suffer now in relation to the world they live in today, but can't say anything about it. They can only explain the today's suffering through yesterday's pain. In the end, their pain remains unexplained.

Suffering which doesn't acquire meaning in words is muffled with medication. Brazil, for example, has reached the top ranking in sales of antidepressants and other anxiolytics. This requires deep reflection from physicians who prescribe these drugs all too often as well as from psychologists who try to explain today's suffering through the suffering of the past and end up leaving suffering itself unexplained. But the situation also calls for reflection by people in general who prefer the easiest solution and the most convenient explanations instead of seeking the true meaning and understanding of their suffering.

011 – WHY DO PEOPLE HAVE SO MUCH MORBID CURIOSITY?

A large amount of people are pleased to see dead bodies, learn about and spread disaster news. Meanwhile, others are pleased to criticize and find this habit ridiculous. Where does our morbid curiosity come from?

In order to define something, we need to compare it with other similar and different things. Thus, if there were only one person in the world who had never been in contact with anyone, he would not be able to define a human being. But we all live surrounded by people, and we have many people to serve as comparison and to help us in defining what a human being is. We define and understand our own humanity by knowing other people and by understanding what exactly a human being is from the comparison we make between their way of existence and ours. However, we only live within our own skin. We can only imagine what goes on inside the skin of others. When our comprehension is reduced to an idea, it is idealized. To measure our own reality, we use an idealized image we make of other people's reality. The criterion that defines reality is the ideal, and we have no other besides it. But this criterion is flawed by principle, because an ideal is opposed to reality by definition.

Within our skin, we live a reality made of flesh and blood. We suffer from weakness, we fear death. We are in constant contact with our own physical and emotional human frailty. Nevertheless, we idealize the human reality of others. We tend to think they don't have the same weaknesses. It's as if we were the only flesh and blood individuals surrounded by a humanity of demigods. Therefore, we also strive to send out to others an idealized image of ourselves. We hide our weaknesses, as they do, in order pass on to them, about us, the same divine image we have of them.

But, there is an unmistakable fragility which is precisely the largest of all. Death appears undisguised. It can be disguised by no one. No one can pass on to others the image of "not being dead". We go through life disguising our mortality, and when death comes, the disguises fall flat. It's in death that people fully reveal they're also made of flesh and blood like us.

The death of others is the opportunity we have to lower the ideal to reality; it is the occasion when we can bridge the gap between the idealized image we have of others and the humanly raw image we have of ourselves. At that moment, we realize that others are

33

made of flesh, like us, and their flesh fades away and ceases to be, as well as our own flesh will cease to be one day.

But just as there are those who delight in lowering the ideal to reality, there are those who delight in raising reality to an ideal. While some seek for frailty and mortality in the semi-divine other, some search themselves for the strength and immortality of the semi-divine other. For these, the realization that the other is a mortal serves as a reminder they are also mortals, something they would rather not have to ever remember. For all that is death-related is dreadful to them, and the morbid curiosity of others is disgusting. Both those who cultivate morbid curiosity and those who are disgusted by it are in conflict with their poor and fragile flesh and blood existence. And there is nothing more human than that.

012 – THERE IS NO SUFFERING HERE AND NOW

The causes of our suffering are related to the future. Those causes identified in the past are also projected onto the future. The memory of a past event signified as loss causes pain today because the loss of the past feels like an absence in the present, and this lack is always accompanied by the desire for it to be compensated or overcome in the future, even when we know it won't be possible. Although the loss is permanent, the desire for compensation remains. In this case, unable to hope for a different future, we wish the past had been different. Still, our desire is linked to the future: a future that has already come and didn't become the present we would've liked it to become. Desire is always future-oriented, even when we desire the past had been different; desire always points to a time which doesn't exist. The difference lies in believing that desired time can still come or knowing the possibility of it coming true has already passed and no longer exists.

Besides desire, fear is another cause for suffering. And just like desire, fear also points to the future. If we are face to face with a hungry lion and we tremble in fear, the cause of fear is not

34

necessarily in the present. Being face to face with a hungry lion is not what causes fear; the real possibility that it will attack at any moment is what frightens us. It's not the present that frightens us; it's the future. And what is fear except the desire for something not to happen?

Desire is the only cause for suffering, and it points to a time which doesn't exist. It points to a past that didn't take place and that exists now as a future which didn't come. It points to a present that is different from the current present and that exists now as the future which didn't become present. It points to a future that never comes and, therefore, it's always the "future" future. However, there is no suffering in the real present, here and now. It is clear that we always experience suffering in the present, but this happens because our thoughts are always tied to a time that's not the immediate present. When we focus on the present moment and current place, we discover that suffering can be everywhere all the time, except here and now. We all have achieved that for a brief moment. Who has never come across a baby and naturally smiled at him, with body and soul? Who has never come face to face with a sudden spectacle of nature and felt, even for a brief moment, totally at peace? These are occasions when our minds can be exactly where our bodies are. These are rare and brief occasions when our thoughts don't wander around times and places other than here and now. These are brief and rare occasions when there's not even a drop of suffering in us.

The reasons that make us suffer are in a time that doesn't exist. Therefore, the causes of suffering don't exist. All there is exists here and now and there's no suffering here and now. Psychoanalysis tells us that we suffer because we've lost the object of our desire a long time ago, and our destiny is to search indefinitely, without ever finding the object once lost. I also think the object will never be found; not because the loss is permanent, but because it never happened. If the loss hasn't occurred, we can stop searching and learn to live here and now. The key to happiness is not in the indefinite pursuit of something that will never be found, but to cease searching for something that doesn't exist and learn to live with what does.

Will that be an easy task? Living here and now is the simplest thing. However, the problem of the simplest things is that we only understand their simplicity after we have accomplished them. For those who still haven't realized the simplicity of the simplest things, it seems nothing can be more difficult. So it is important not to be deceived by the apparent difficulty. Just remember that the difficulties are never in the present, but rather projected onto a time that doesn't exist. Thus, they do not exist.

013 – THOSE WHO DREAM, DO NOT LIVE

I believe it's the psychologist's job to criticize those easy truths, so full of romanticism, to which we cling so easily and repeat to the four winds without thinking, and which place us so far from an authentic life. Among them, one of the strongest is that which advocates the value of dreams and the importance of never give up on them. "Those who don't dream, don't live"; "Never stop dreaming"; "Never give up on your dreams". Who has never read, heard, repeated or shared such statements as if it were life's greatest truth?

Our society is dream-addicted. Of course, adult life requires us to execute projects and to have at least minimal concerns about the future. But this somewhat objective concern about the future doesn't mean that future possibilities should become the meaning of our life and our main driving force. After all, if dreams are that which give life meaning, what will become of us in old age, when there's not enough time and possibilities to fulfill any more dreams? How will we solve the "meaning of life" issue when we're old?

There is only one reason for so much dreaming: Dissatisfaction with what we are and what we have in the present. Those who spend their whole life dreaming, starting one project after another without ever ceasing to dream, live an entirely unfulfilled life. They never stop dreaming and start living. What good would our dreams be if we were really happy in the present? However, those who never stop dreaming, those who live and pass on that "dream philosophy", are always in high spirits, always cultivating "positive thinking". These are people who refuse to see that which displeases them. They interpret losses and mishaps as "necessary steps" in the way of success and achievement; they see a door that closes as the announcement of two windows opening. They see the way down the hill as an opportunity to accelerate back up. Those who live in a constant dream are afflicted with a chronic optimism that prevents them from recognizing and naturally accepting life's natural and inevitable sorrows, and by that they become unable to realize that their own lives have become a deep regret.

The driving force behind their optimism is anxiety; anxiety about things that can't be controlled now; anxiety about the future they can't ensure. Anxiety is the fire that keeps their balloon flying high above the ground of reality, in constant struggle with the gravity that pulls it into the abyss of depression. Our dreaming society is also the most depressed. Many people can't take the thin air of the heights of chronic optimism, and become depressed as dead weights on the hard ground of reality.

The higher the flight of chronic optimism, the shorter will be the breath to overcome adversity. And when it's no longer possible to deny the breathlessness of anguish, depression will be the inevitable end. Optimism, which should make people stronger, weakens them. And the depression which they wanted to avoid with optimism eventually becomes an even more real threat. The force required to overcome adversity and achieve dreams is given to us by the ability to live awakened in the reality of now. Those who live in a dream never wake up for life, and it is in waking life that dreams can come true. So let us stop dreaming and start living.

014 – THERE IS NO CHANGE WITHOUT SELF-ACCEPTANCE

Many people seek a psychologist because they want to change something in themselves. They come dissatisfied with what they are and what they do, and hope the psychologist will help transform them. The intended change, although viable, turns out to be a complicated process because people in therapy find it hard to understand a very paradoxical truth: You can't change yourself without accepting yourself.

This truth, however, though paradoxical, is quite obvious: people who want to change something in themselves do not like what they are. Consequently, their self-esteem is low. They want to feel good about themselves, but to do so they would have to accept themselves the way they are. People usually understand this part of the reasoning easily; they know that in order to feel good about themselves they need self-acceptance; but they have one condition: "Before I can accept myself, I have to change that which displeases me about myself".

There is plenty of illusion in this way of thinking. People who want to change themselves think of their own "self" as if it were a thing or an object that they could change on their own. It's as if they were at the same time the acting subjects and the objects acted upon. But the objects acted upon don't exist; there're only subjects. In this case, subject and object are the same thing. Anyone who tries to change himself is groping the air; they act upon a non-existing object, and a non-existing object can't be modified. Consequently, they will go on not achieving the desired change and will continue without accepting themselves as they are.

People who wish to accept themselves as they are have one condition for that: they must first apply a few changes. By doing so, they become victims of an illusion and a paradox: they believe the possibility of changing an object that doesn't exist and want to accept themselves as long as they're different. This paradox puts them in a difficult situation and they can't realize it because they're trapped in the illusion that it's possible to solve it!

Change cannot be a condition for self-acceptance. Acceptance must take place unconditionally. And when acceptance occurs, a second illusion vanishes: A person who wants to change himself believes change and acceptance are two different actions. But when acceptance takes place, change occurs simultaneously. Self-acceptance is the change itself, not the condition for change to occur. Those who want to no longer be shy learn that accepting their own shyness means setting aside the embarrassment for being shy and by that... they stop being shy! Those who want to become less jealous discover that accepting their own jealousy and stop suffering because of it actually means... give up on jealousy! These who feel lonely and want to make more friends or find a loving partner discover that, by accepting their own loneliness, they lose the fear of being alone; losing their fear of being alone, they stop surrounding themselves with defenses which prevented them from being hurt or abandoned again by also keeping them away from people and... lonely!

Expressions such as "change", "growth", and "transformation", when applied to personal development, are metaphorical and misleading. They all have a meaning linked to the idea of "movement" but, when taken literally, they lead us to the opposite state, stagnation. There is no growth, change, or transformation. Maturity occurs only in knowing and accepting what we already are.

015 – WHY DO WE WANT TO BE USEFUL?

Our society lives the utilitarianism disease. We only attribute value to what can be useful. When faced with something unknown, the first question we ask is "What is the use of that?" Usefulness and utility became the fundamental criteria of the value we attribute to something. Something useless is dispensable, it has no meaning. Therefore, we seek the meaning of things in their utility. But what escapes our understanding is that we only seek the meaning of the most important things in their utility when we're unable to understand their real meaning.

According to Aristotle, utility is a means, not the end. Cutlery is useful because it serves for eating, and therein lies their value. However, what is more important: the silverware or what they are used for? Of course, eating is more important than the silverware. Cutlery is only important because it serves for eating. Similarly, all useful things are less important than what they are used for. Thus, the most important things are useless. Those things are good in themselves.

Among the most important things, the most important of all is life. All useful things are only useful in terms of making our life happy. Life should be good in itself, because there's nothing more important than life. And so that life can be good in itself, we need to find its true meaning, which is no easy task. In the difficulty of finding a real meaning for life, we try to compensate its lack of sense by giving it a utility. The ever frequent pursuit of a use for life is a symptom of how many people live a meaningless life... and don't even realize it!

The meaning of a useful thing is in something that is different from itself. The meaning of silverware is not the silverware itself, but eating. And so it is with everything else. But how can we find a use for existence? The existence embraces everything. Thus, a useful existence is useful in relation to what? Useful existence can only be useful in relation to itself. So people searching for a use for existence turn their life into a continuous "doing". They are always "doing something", they are always "producing", always "active". But what exactly are they doing? What are they producing? It doesn't matter! What matters is doing and producing, no matter what! The medium is more important than the end. For these people, existence must be useful in relation to itself. So existence must be an ongoing activity whose function is solely... "doing" the existence! Therefore, their existence finds no rest... finds no peace!

Life isn't useful in relation to anything. Life is good in itself. Thus, the meaning of life cannot be given by its utility. Life has no utility. It can't be the means to do or produce life itself. Life is its own purpose; life is an end in itself. If life becomes the means to produce life itself, its meaning is lost. The meaning of life is found only in the stillness, the quiet, the silence. But it is precisely in the stillness that we realize life's lack of utility. And that emptiness, which should be full of meaning, is experienced as anguish. Anguish soon turns into anxiety, and then comes the thought "I have to get up and do something!".

We want to be useful because we haven't learned to live and let life be. We can't make our existence satisfied with itself; we need to make it useful for something; and since this "something" is existence itself, we're like mad dogs, chasing their own tails, using life to "do" life itself. It would be much easier to just live! But the easiest things are also the hardest and the simplest are also the most complicated to understand.

016 – THE FEAR OF GETTING INVOLVED IS PROPORTIONAL TO THE FEAR OF LOSING

Much is said about how ephemeral relationships today are. Nostalgics of a recent past say relationships some time ago were more stable, perhaps forgetting that such stability didn't necessarily indicate happiness. However, if some current relationships are more transient, others have gotten more serious, and sometimes last much longer than they should if they were healthy.

Dating today is a serious thing. When a couple is officially dating, it means the relationship became serious, and stability is expected of a serious relationship. The invention of commitment rings attributed a meaning to dating that only marriage had. Dating is no longer a relationship that serves to get to know the other person better. Actually, that "get to know one another" meaning isn't completely lost; it only had an additional meaning added to it. While a few decades ago this "get to know the partner" meant a relationship that could end at any moment or last for a long time, people nowadays want to be assured it will last a long time in order to get involved.

If there is no guarantee that the relationship will be stable, people don't feel comfortable getting involved. A few decades ago, this guarantee didn't exist; it used to be built along the couple's history, and yet no one saw obstacles in getting involved. People used to get involved without worrying too much about the future, and if the relationship ended, the two involved were free to date again and get involved again. Of course I speak in general terms. People have never been so "well settled". But the principle I am discussing was true: There was no guarantee of stability in dating, and yet people got involved, even if it meant they would suffer later.

People today are more afraid to get involved. Therefore, they need an assurance or the illusion of one. The commitment ring is one of the symbols of this illusion. However, people who are most afraid to get involved are precisely the most afraid of losing their partners after already being involved, even if the relationship makes them unhappy. Consequently, they tend to hold the partner and preserve the relationship at all costs. The relationship only ends when one can no longer look on the other's face. Ironically, stability symbolized by the ring ends up being conquered, but its price is much greater than the suffering previously feared.

Those who aren't free to get involved aren't free to let go of that with which they're involved. Those looking for assurances in order to get involved end up turning involvement into an addiction, and addiction is a source of much more suffering than the amount of suffering that could be avoided by letting go. Some relationships today are puerile and ephemeral because people no longer trust anyone. They believe there's a tendency that others will abandon them. But they don't trust one another precisely because they don't trust their own ability to overcome the end of a relationship and move on. And those who have so much fear will inevitably project them onto others: "The threat comes from others, not from myself." In turn, some relationships today are long and immature because they're based on dependency, not involvement. Even a dating relationship of a few months sometimes appears to be as worn as a marriage that is decades old, and the couple still does everything to preserve it, as if their commitment ring had been forged with blood! Mature affection is one that is free to get involved and free to let go. It seems that neither our generation nor the generation of nostalgics of the past managed to understand this very well.

017 – THE OPRESSION OF LAUGHTER

Freud wrote that laughter releases the tension of that which is repressed in us. A trained and educated man laughs at everything that presents in a derogatory manner whatever constrains his values and morality. Laughter releases tension suppressed by allowing the repressed to be depreciated. Thus, if on the one hand laughter frees us of repressed tension, on the other hand it keeps us prisoners of what's repressed, since depreciation is a form of separation – or repression – of what is embarrassing to us. A man's main laughing object is himself. We laugh at a behavior that seems ridiculous to us, and we also laugh at the behavior which, even though seems lovely to us, is judged as inappropriate to our age and status. An adult man laughs at children in order to keep a prisoner within himself the child he still is. At family gatherings, the child surrounded by aunts, grandparents and cousins becomes a circus attraction and all laugh out loud at the show of a child who's only doing what every child does ever since the world began. A child doesn't laugh at another child, and the man who finds grace in children is not a free man. Free is the man who looks at children as naturally as they look one another, as if he was one of them himself.

We live in the society of laughter. Few things are as cultivated in our midst as the easy laugh. In social life, the first rule is: Laugh and make others laugh. The second rule is: If you are unable to make others laugh, at least laugh. Laughter is convenient because it frees us from the tension involved in our relationship with others while reinforcing the values and principles which keep this relationship in oppression, and which we still don't wish to abandon. Therefore, to make people laugh is the best way to win their sympathy, and the criteria we use to assess the way others accept us is how much we can make them laugh with us at the things we say. Receiving laughter as a response is very rewarding, and so we understand that others also expect the same reward we do. Seriousness is not welcome. We say we seek faithful, loyal, and honest people. Faithfulness, loyalty, and honesty are values, and the cultivation of such values requires that they be treated seriously. But if you place someone faithful, loyal, honest – and serious – on your right and someone unfaithful, disloyal, dishonest

– and funny – on your left, you will note that the person on your right will stand alone and that people will gather as a swarm of bees around the person on your left.

Laughing and making others laugh is almost an etiquette rule. Those who can neither laugh nor make others laugh at people's foolishness will be isolated, and will probably suffer difficulties in social interaction, even if they're faithful, loyal, and honest people. Indeed, their seriousness will be an obstacle for others to know better about their deepest virtues. In turn, those who are skilled in laughing and making others laugh are likely to become a prisoner of the role they play. Everybody expects them to laugh at any nonsense they hear and, chiefly, everybody expects these people to always make them laugh – a lot! Moreover, it's possible that the ease of gaining the sympathy of many people by laughter will make them addicted to it and so they don't develop the seriousness that all relationships require. Consequently, a person with this behavior can become superficial: a person who's popular and knows a lot of people but can't become truly intimate with anyone.

The obligation to laugh and make others laugh is oppressive for those who can't carry it out and for those who perform it masterfully. The result is a society that is futile and governed by the appearances we all criticize, but also desire and build with absolute conviction! Because all we really want is a good laugh!

018 – WHAT DOESN'T KILL YOU MAKES YOU WEAKER

"What doesn't kill you makes you stronger". Who has never heard or repeated that? This premise is part of our current "popular wisdom". It is obviously not true when it comes to organic disorders. People who go through illnesses don't come out of them stronger, but weakened. Their poor health will inspire care for some time. Health is what strengthens the body, not disease. It would be absurd to think otherwise. So why would psychological distress strengthen us? Are people who constantly undergo severe losses or disappointments in life stronger than those who live happy all the time? Organic illness is a warning that the body is vulnerable, and disease makes it even more weakened, even when it develops the necessary defenses for the cure during recovery. The same applies to "illness" of the soul. Suffering is a sign that our affectivity isn't right, and episodes of great pain make us even more vulnerable. There are some diseases that make us immune to a relapse. Was the jargon of common sense inspired in this kind of occurrence to convince us that, after heartbreak, for example, we become immune to new disappointments? Do people strive to believe in that when they repeat that jargon from the rooftops?

It's so hard to naturally accept life's inevitable sorrows! We have a great need to find positive meaning in suffering; to find gain in all losses. It's hard to accept that loss is just loss and live peacefully with that fact. Ironically, it's by accepting loss with serenity and resignation that we grow stronger to face future losses. Those who try to give every loss a sense of gain or try to attribute a strengthening sense to pain episodes are only applying to suffer again in the future, as well as those who think they're stronger after flu increase their chances of having a relapse. Those who think suffering makes people stronger are seeking for a sense in it and those seeking for a sense in suffering end up cultivating and perpetuating it. It's a contradiction: It is believed that the path of suffering will lead to non-suffering and that by suffering we learn to suffer no more.

Buddha realized there was no use whatsoever in suffering and that therefore we should abandon it. Suffering does have its good side: we don't need it for anything. We learn to stop suffering when we start seeing it naturally as regret, not when we cultivate its "good" side. The cultivation of suffering reaches the top when people say "I needed to go through it". The maximum cultivation of suffering means believing that suffering is necessary; it means believing that suffering can be useful! A strong person is someone who goes through life's inevitable losses and disappointments naturally and without having to be convinced that there's a bright side to the whole situation. Those who only endure suffering by believing in its "good" side show their inability to deal with it; and the most unable to cope with grief naturally are just the ones who suffer most.

45

In short, suffering only makes us stronger when we don't try to give it a sense of strengthening. Those who realize their own weaknesses without using them as excuses to avoid life and not trying to pretend they no longer exist, lose the fear of suffering. And those who learn to naturally receive suffering kill its seed! Imagining strength where there's only weakness can give us a momentary good mood, but it makes us even weaker when we have to deal with further losses in the future. And accumulating losses without receiving them naturally makes us increasingly vulnerable, while our illusory strength only increases... That's where people start to post these self-deception white lies such as "what doesn't kill me makes me stronger".

019 – JEALOUSY ENCOURAGES CHEATING

You know that afflicted and worried mother who's always making recommendations and giving advice to her teen children? She makes a huge mistake: with her anxiety, she conveys the message that she's the one who has the most to lose if something bad happens, not the child. This message triggers the following unconscious reasoning in the child's mind: "If my mother is the one who has the most to lose with my attitudes, she is the one responsible for preventing me to do something wrong. Consequently, if she can't prevent me from behaving badly, so what I'm doing shouldn't be that wrong or dangerous. If it were, she would find a way to stop me". This reasoning is based on a very elementary unconscious fantasy: if there is someone who cares about us, even if that someone is away, that person's concern protects us and makes us immune to the life's dangers. Isn't that fantasy similar to our trust in God? Anyway, the most recommended and advised children are usually very mischievous. And, deep down, they test life's dangers because they feel protected by the concern of those who love them.

Something similar occurs with jealousy. A jealous person conveys the message that he is the one who has the most to lose with the partner's possible cheating. Consequently, the partner unconsciously starts the following reasoning: "the jealous one is who has the most to lose if I cheat, so he wants to control everything I do. But if the jealous one controls my behavior, the responsibility for what I do is entirely hiss. The one in control always holds the responsibility". The unconscious fantasy that the cheating has the jealous' consent is based on this reasoning and so those who consent to cheating become responsible for it. The unconscious fantasy coexists with the conscious knowledge that the jealous may not forgive the cheater, leave his partner or even resort to aggression. But the dispute between conscious knowledge and unconscious fantasy is disproportionate! For example, even though we can be sincerely aware that death may come at any moment, we never truly believe that. Deep down, we always believe in immortality.

Anyone dominated by the unconscious fantasy that betrayal has the partner's consent will show greater tendency to betray than those who didn't develop this fantasy – even if that fantasy antagonizes with their principles and conscious desires. And a key factor in the development of this fantasy is the jealousy of those who fear betrayal.

In view of the jealous' controlling behavior, betrayal can be understood as the partner's self-affirmation that says, "I am in control of what I do, not you". This understanding is correct. But subsequent analysis shows that, if on the one hand the partner wants to regain control of his life with betrayal, on the other hand he chooses betrayal precisely in view of the controlling behavior of the jealous partner: "It was his control that led me to betray him". The responsibility for betrayal is transferred to the jealous, and the responsible for the action always consents to it. We arrive, thus, at the same point.

If mothers could only inform their children about the dangers of life without transmitting them excessive anxiety, kids would swallow dry and understand that they hold full responsibility for their own actions. Similarly, if partners would demonstrate trust in each other and mutually convey the message that everyone is responsible for what they do, the weight of a betrayal would be more intensely felt by the person thinking of cheating, and chances

47

are it would happen less. Of course there are people who would betray in any situation, and this only serves to remind us that the lesson to be learned from all this is that you can't control the behavior of an adult. So let us relax and take care of our own actions – because we are the only ones responsible for them and for them only.

020 – THE DARKEST SIDE OF OUR NORMALITY

When the media reports news of a massacre, a serial killer, or any other brutal murder crime, common-sense rushes to classify the author of the crime as "sick", "maniac" or "mad". A contradictory tendency reveals itself in people in general: While they express a desire to understand the causes or motivations that lead someone to commit heinous crimes, in their understanding effort lies the desire to eliminate as soon as possible their identification with the author of these crimes. They portray such criminals as exceptions or cases where elements not present in normality determine the criminals' conduct. The concept of "illness" is the key. Mental illness is seen as abnormal functioning of the mind whose cause is a foreign element of impersonal origin, something that is not found in normal people and that only comes in determining someone's behavior for very specific and rare reasons.

In our society, "violence" is synonymous with "fun". Our film heroes are killers who boldly fight, kill and die. Clearly, there's always a "noble cause" behind the carnage. But who cares, really? That's not what makes them glorious. Otherwise, pacifists such as Gandhi and Mother Theresa would be the heroes of our youth instead of pumped Hollywood actors. The cause for which they fight is not what makes them heroes, but the fact that they're able to annihilate their enemies one by one, with cruelty, and still make an ironic comment before their last breath. No psychopath would do better! From very young ages, our children play war games in which the goal is to shoot as many enemy soldiers as they can. The blood that almost literally splashes from the TV screen is pleasing

48

to them. They are taught early that mangling other people is fun. After all, it's all "make believe", it doesn't hurt!

Violence exists within us. But we don't realize it because we strive to believe that we only enjoy the "make-believe" type of violence, and that therefore our violent nature also exists in a "make-believe" way in us. Then, when someone goes around shooting at people in schools, it disturbs us to realize that the make-believe violence within us is quite real. "How could that happen?", we ask astonished. "Violence was supposed to be just for fun! This guy didn't understand anything! He's certainly ill!". But perhaps he is the one who has understood it all and we still haven't understood a thing. Perhaps he's the one who has understood that the violence within himself is quite real, whereas we still strive to believe that it is nothing but an innocent pastime. Violence is our dark side; it's part of that nature that we don't recognize as "ours"; part of that side of us which lies in darkness and we can't see clearly. We lack familiarity with our dark side. And so it penetrates our attitudes and our way of being before we can realize it. So when we see it revealed so clearly and objectively on someone else, our reaction is repulsion. We don't understand it, we don't accept it. We refuse to believe that something like that is part of "normality". Violence is the dark side of normality, and it hides from normality by crawling deeply into it. Similarly, normality flirts with illness which manifests itself slyly in the form of an innocent taste for scenic blood.

Those who don't know their own nature are eventually controlled by it. The forces we ignore within us end up controlling us like puppets – and we ultimately blame the world, society, the media, etc., for everything. Violence which manifests itself clearly and objectively in psychopaths is also manifested in ourselves not only in the taste for make-believe violence, but in socially accepted forms of violence such as "pranks" between adults or other behavior patterns that reproduce the loneliness and misery of our human relationships. The wide recognition of this fact is the first step toward change.

Every child wakes up in the middle of the night crying after having dreamt that mom and dad died. The same way children grow up fast and their clothes become too small, they also grow mature quickly, and the dependency on their parents makes them uncomfortable. Dependency is always oppressive and oppression is always distressing. There's a natural tendency in us to push away any object of anxiety. But children's love for their parents usually overshadows the anguish and prevents them from experiencing it. That which is not experienced while they're awake appears in their dreams, and the desire to push away the parents who are the source of their anxiety is manifested in dreams in which the parents die.

If on the one hand the relationship with parents is a source of anguish, on the other hand it is a source of satisfaction because the child loves them and finds great fulfillment in being with them. Thus, the sum of the desire to get away from them with the desire to stay with them results in the need to mature the relationship established with them. The current relationship of dependency has to "die" to be reborn matching the child's current level of maturity. That's the need represented in the dream. The coexistence of the desire to get away from someone and the desire to remain with them doesn't occur without conflict. This conflict may be evident while children are awake, through the fear of losing their parents. And the fear of losing them can appear as the fear they might die or the fear of being abandoned by them.

There are people who live fearing abandonment of those they love even though they never went through such an experience and even though their partners haven't shown any desire to abandon them. These people tend to establish dependency relationships, that is, immature relationships for their condition. And their immaturity doesn't manifest itself only through dependency, but also through their inability to properly deal with the conflict arising from it. Indeed, those who can't accept the inner desire to get away from those they love will transform that desire into a source of guilt and remorse. They'll doubt the legitimacy and veracity of

50

their love and suffer because of that. Consequently, it's natural that we repress every desire to move away from our loved ones, and that which is repressed inevitably ends up being projected onto others. So the person who wants to get away from someone and represses that desire will live haunted by the thought that his loved one is the one who wants to get away from them.

When the desire to get away from a loved one is unconscious, in the fantasy that comes along with it we attribute to our loved one the knowledge of that desire. Unconsciously, we attribute to everyone the knowledge of what is unconscious in us. And the desire to abandon our partner, which awakens remorse in us, would arouse resentment in them, once it was known by them. We wish to abandon them; so they're resentful and want revenge by leaving us too. And there are plenty of cases in which the person who fears being abandoned is the one who, in fact, abandons his beloved. Because of the fear of being abandoned, which is so real to them, they abandon first in order not to be abandoned. The inability to deal with the conflict between the desire to get away and the desire to remain with the partner, which should be resolved by maturing the relationship, forces us to abandon the ones we love, since the ghost of abandonment has made it unsustainable to stay together. Dependency poses a dilemma: Both remaining with the loved one and getting away from them are distressing options. Therefore, dependent people are divided into two groups: Those who can't be steady with a partner and those who cling to them obsessively and live haunted by fantasies of abandonment and betrayal.

022 – THE CONDITIONS TO UNCONDITIONAL LOVE

Trust is magical. There's no logic to it. We learn to trust people from the cradle and continue to trust as adults based on intuition. Defenseless children realize that there's a world around them that does everything to meet their needs. Over time, they understand that their survival depends on this world and that this world is made of people like themselves. If children's existence depends on other people, these people are for children the very essence of their existence. The people surrounding them are the foundation these children's lives depend on. But a foundation's sole meaning is to give support. Therefore, if on one hand the people around these children are the most important part of themselves, on the other hand they exist only to support them and meet their needs. And this is how children learn what love is. From the depths of their self-centeredness, they delegate to the people they love the most important place in their lives, but also expect them to satisfy their needs. This expectation doesn't manifest itself only when they cry, make tantrum and require immediate attention, but also in the naive trust that makes them give their hand to any adult who approaches them, because they believes that everyone is there for their sake. Love is the product of our self-centeredness. But who ever said that self-centeredness can't be as pure and sweet as the love of a child?

Trust brings the expectation that the people around us will fulfill what we expect of them; and expectation is the mother of all disappointments. This expectation is one side of the love coin; the other, as previously said, is to give people we love the most important place in our lives. Consequently, the frustration of that expectation may undermine both our ability to love and the capacity to get involved in any kind of relationship. Trust is essential in order to love and to relate to others. If people don't meet what we expect of them, it's hard to love and establish relationships with them. How do we learn to love and relate ignoring so many breaches of trust?

Love is the manifestation of our self-centeredness; our most childish, pure, and naive self-centeredness. Thus, there's no such thing as unconditional love. There's no love or relationship without expectations. People who love unconditionally are those who learn to overcome their disappointments, because they're inevitable and they'll exist as long as there is a relationship – any kind of relationship. Those who learn to love unconditionally are able to see their childish egocentrism from a new perspective, although it is impossible to eliminate it. Whereas children believe that it is the world's duty to quench their needs, an adult person should understand that he is the one responsible for delegating this duty to others and to the world, and also for the resulting disappointments. Each one of us is solely responsible for what we feel, unlike what tells us the famous phrase of Antoine de Saint-Exupéry.

When adults understand that they hold full responsibility for the obligations they delegate to others, they learn to trust what they feel for other people instead of trusting what they expect from them. And so, through logical paths they finally learn what unconditional love is. Unconditional love is not the love without conditions; it is the love that learns to disdain the conditions put to love, since there would be no love if these conditions hadn't been placed. It is love that plays silly, and goes on loving without conditions as if it were conditional. Unconditional love is playful love.

023 – WHY DO WE FEEL CONTROLED BY OTHERS?

No one possesses power. Power is always a concession of those subordinated to it. Once granted, the power is exercised, never possessed. Human relations are relations of power. All those involved in a relationship control, in one way or another, each other. People engage in relationships, whether romantic or strictly professional, because it's in relationships that they find satisfaction for their multiple needs. If it weren't possible to control human relationships directing them to the satisfaction of our needs, no one would get involved. And if the possibility of satisfaction depends on the ability to control the world and other people, then even babies are able to control and exercise the power granted to them.

This truth can be attest by any mother. Children who cry and receive the attention of those who take care of them as a response soon learns that crying has its positive consequences. They start to cry whenever they need something, and the cry becomes the instrument by which they control the world around them. This is where their education must start. Education operates precisely by countercontrol. When parents refuse to promptly respond to their child's requests, they begin to establish conditions to the child's satisfaction. Children who have the satisfaction of their needs conditioned learn to distinguish those critical from those that aren't essential and also learn to delay the relief of all of them when necessary. Ironically, the learning of indirect paths to satisfaction is also used as an instrument of control. If children understand the conditions established in order for them to get what they want, they'll exploit that knowledge to try to modify them and to take as much of the world as possible. And so, the world will again exercise its countercontrol, and the learning relationship will extend for life.

The exercise of control always gets some kind of countercontrol as a response. So why do so many people find themselves suffocated in their relationships? They feel out of room, completely controlled either by their bosses, their parents, or loving partners. Strictly speaking, the countercontrol exercised over them isn't smaller than the control they exercise themselves, but they feel as if they didn't exert any control and as if they were fully controlled by the circumstances. The countercontrol exercised over us by the world is a dangerous thing: it can lead us to the conclusion that accepting the conditions imposed on us is safer than trying to change them; that is, we often learn that accepting conditions imposed is the safest way to control the possibility of negative consequences. Thus, people who accept all the conditions imposed on them in their relationships control the negative consequences of their actions: they know that attempting to modify these conditions may cause them great harm when they result in adverse reactions of others. By avoiding confrontation they avoid such consequences, and avoiding is a way of controlling. However, the ends are always equal: the huge effort to avoid negative consequences reveals itself as an extreme impotence in avoiding them. People who try to control negative consequences by accepting all adverse conditions will be completely controlled by them, and there can be no negative consequence worse than being completely controlled by adverse conditions. Being completely controlled by adverse conditions is the cause for the feeling of oppression and powerlessness, which is merely the result of extreme control exercising over the chances of suffering negative consequences. Those who want to feel in control of their lives must give up control over the world. We must be subjected to possibilities beyond our control if we are to expand the possibilities of having what we want under our control. In other words, as common sense wisely goes, "Nothing ventured, nothing gained".

024 – OLD AGE IS NOT A SECOND CHILDHOOD

Do we know how to grow old? Old age is supposed to be "the third age" which follows childhood and adulthood. However, watching our seniors I come to the conclusion that old age is more like a return to childhood. On one hand, we have examples of seniors who wind up full of fears and foibles, who demand more and more attention and end up losing the ability to transit through worldly affairs. These are precisely the ones who end up being infantilized and treated as children. However, on the other hand we have examples of those who preserve their lucidity and autonomy, and live actively, but sometimes squander what seems to be a puerile, childish joy. The media appreciates this second type of people. I usually call them "Entertainment Show Seniors"; those old people who appear on TV stories living and behaving as if they weren't elderly, and whose image is sold to us as the ideal old age paradigm.

And we buy that image. We end up convincing ourselves that the best old age is the one in which we live as if we weren't old. We don't stop to think that, in this attitude, old age means something negative: the best way to be old is to deny old age; it's to live as if we were still young. Our seniors thus face a dilemma: They can't be old, because old age is bad; and they can't enjoy adulthood's freedom and possibilities, since they are limited by their fragile health conditions and body weaknesses. All they can do is migrate back to childhood! And there we have both those who become children and distance themselves from the world and those who become children and live the world intensely!

The joy of living is obviously a good thing. But when we use it to compensate for our inability to deal with our own conflicts, it becomes as childish and artificial as the joy of the drunk. Those who can't accept an inevitable condition such as old age live in conflict with it and can't delve deeper. And the result of such shallow experience is old age that looks like everything but old age; old age that looks exactly like its opposite, a childhood full of the most childish joy.

We buy the idea that we should be young forever; young not only in physical appearance but also in our living attitude. And we confuse a life that is active and full of laughter with the life of those who remain forever young. However, people who are active and full of laughter are generally those that are still in their young years. And aging affects only that which is preserved in the same condition for a long time. Indefinitely preserving a young person's attitude to life until old age doesn't mean preserving youth; it means becoming immature. Immaturity affects those who preserve the attitude of an age that is no longer theirs beyond time; and there is no worse form of old age than immaturity. The preservation of youth requires renovation. And the renewal that we are discussing here means precisely setting aside adulthood to become old in body and soul. Young is an elderly man who's not afraid to be old.

Where are the wise fairy tale seniors with so many life lessons to teach us? Unfortunately, they are increasingly only found in those stories. And since the cult of eternal youth is much larger for our generation than it was for the generation of people who are older now, I fear greatly for the type of old people we will become. If it's already harder and harder to leave the teen years and become an adult, we are probably close to the day when the true old people will live only in fairy tales.

025 – WHY IS IT SO HARD TO OVERCOME HURT?

Hurt is the permanent feeling of having our ego depreciated by others. We regularly experience similar feelings that go by unnoticed and don't necessarily turn into hurt. Depreciation felt repeatedly or felt every time a painful event is remembered characterizes hurt. However, an event remembered doesn't always cause us hurt. Though painful, the devaluation sense may be attributed to the event only when it is remembered for the first time, or rather once after many other recollections. That sense can also be attributed to an event whose original experience wasn't painful. The act of re-feeling an event can give it a sense of devaluation of the ego. Thus, the cause of hurt is never the original experience, but the re(-)sent(i)ment. It is the resentment that brings the feeling of devaluation experienced in a painful event; it also creates that feeling even when the original experience is absent from it. Therefore, hurt is the product of a judging process in which an event is analyzed repeatedly and gradually signified as the occurrence of an insult.

Ego is its own judging instance. Freud divided it into "ego" and "superego", giving superego the role of ego's judging instance. Ego is only judged by itself. Therefore, any depreciation of the ego comes from ego itself. But in hurt, we feel that our ego has been depreciated by others. The experience of a feeling is always a passive one. The feeling is our own, but we have no control over initiating it, ending it or defining its intensity and tone. If we cannot control any of that, we can be easily confused in judging and attributing to others the responsibility of having caused us our own feelings with their actions and words. Thus, when we feel undervalued, we identify the cause as the actions and words of those who "devalue" us and identify them as offenders.

We accuse others of offending us, but this accusation is a consequence of the fact that we devalue ourselves. Hurt is a consequence of the ego not accepting itself in conditions considered depreciative by ego itself. This refusal comes from ego itself, for whom other people's actions and words create unacceptable conditions for the acceptance of itself. Still, ego blames someone else for its own hurt when no one besides itself has judged it, depreciated it, and put it through the humiliation of rejection. Others are responsible for their own actions. If they make mistakes, they should be held responsible, legally even, if that's the case. But ego's own self-rejection is its own responsibility. Although others might intend to depreciate us with their actions and words, none of that would work if we wouldn't consider it depreciative. Attributing a depreciative sense to other people's actions and words is giving them means to devalue us, and we alone are the ones responsible for that. Hurt is the product of ego's judgement of itself, and no one else can be accounted for it. Because even if someone else is held responsible and wishes to make it up to us, how could he do that? Hurt disappears only when the ego is at peace with itself; only when the ego reviews and erases the derogatory judgment on itself. If it doesn't review its judgment, there's nothing other people can do. It is the ego's ultimate decision to feel hurt and no one else's.

Hurt is hard to overcome because we insist on attributing to others a judgment we inflict on ourselves and which only we can appeal and reconsider. Hurt is hard to overcome because we spend a long time expecting a payment for something that can't be paid. And if it can't be paid, then the debt doesn't exist! People who hurt us owe us nothing. They must be held responsible for their actions, certainly; but the "debt" for the egoic wound, for which we insist on charging them, they can't pay. And they can't pay for it because this isn't their "debt"; the debt is ours and only we can pay it off.

When we think of overcoming hurt, we imagine a number of conditions that should be met: compensation actions for those who hurt us, long periods of "personal growth", etc. There is no need for any of these conditions. Ego is independent and it doesn't depend on any condition to judge or to cancel that judgement. The difficulty lies precisely in understanding that.

026 – SHAME IS OUR WORST ENEMY

Shame comes when weakness is laid bare. It accompanies the feeling that our most reprehensible intimacy is exposed. People often have dreams in which they are naked in public. These dreams fulfill our desire to overcome the oppressive censorship that we impose on ourselves and to reveal to the world all that which we hold deep within us in so much fear. So when something that was kept deep within is revealed to the world, we want to disappear into the depth from which it came. When we feel ashamed and we have nowhere to run, our desire is to escape into ourselves and disappear.

Some people frequently use the expression "to die of shame". What hardly anyone knows is that shame actually kills a lot of people. In few occasions we are able to experience our fragility and our lack of sufficiency as deeply as in serious accidents. In the few seconds of a tragedy, lots of thoughts go through your head. Among them, we experience like never the fact that our existence is entirely sustained by conditions we don't control and that can change suddenly unbeknownst to us. The abrupt and strong exposure of a sense of fragility previously unknown makes us want to disappear within ourselves, there where this feeling has always been hidden. That's the true reason for some accident survivors to slip into coma and sometimes even die. Not to mention the countless people who, although didn't suffer any serious accident, die of a heart attack or other complications in similar exposure situations.

However, shame is an enemy that attacks us more often than we imagine. If it wasn't for shame, no one would suffer for being alone. Loneliness is also experienced as exposure of our weakness to the world. When we are alone we feel insecure, we have no one to support us. And insofar as everybody knows we are alone (and we always imagine that everybody knows that we are alone), we feel that our frailty is exposed. Shame accompanies this sense of exposure. Loneliness hurts because we feel ashamed of being alone. The suffering caused by loneliness is founded in shame, and shame accompanies the sense of fragility. But those who are able to understand this soon realize that our greatest weakness is shame itself, that by leaving it aside we suppress the fragility of being alone and the very anguish of loneliness, consequently. The same goes for other conditions to which we are exposed, such as being unemployed or acquiring a disability. Besides the practical difficulties we may face, the suffering these conditions cause is based on the shame we feel when others see us going through such conditions. Nobody wants to be seen as unemployed or disabled. Being seen in these conditions means exposing our weaknesses or our failure. And the shame we feel about that is what leads us to depression, bitterness or stagnation.

Many interpret shame as a result of low self-esteem. What many people still don't realize is that low self-esteem is a result of pride and vanity. Only vain and proud people suffer from low self-esteem. If someone proud and vain wants to be or appear to be better than he actually is, then what he really is will be a reason for low self-esteem. Pride and low self-esteem are always two sides of the same coin: When one manifests itself openly, the other manifests itself implicitly. So the shame of what we are and what we keep hidden from everyone is a result of our pride, and all pride is silly! Abandoning shame doesn't mean exchanging it for proud self-affirmation, but putting aside the need for self-affirmation. Because shame is the effect of the failure of our self-affirmation before the world.

027 – SANTA CLAUS, THANKS FOR NOT BEING REAL!

So goes a page from the diary I wrote as a child:

"Christmas day, 1984:

The celebration was great. I got lots of gifts. I felt emotional. It was a good party. I ate so much! I almost cried. It was a great Christmas. Because I already know that Santa Claus doesn't exist."

When I was a child, Santa Claus fascinated me. His existence was so wonderfully absurd that I couldn't help but fill my imagination with assumptions and questions. I asked many questions about Santa Claus. I wanted to understand how he managed to travel around the world in one night carrying gifts for all children on

Earth not forgetting anyone's name, completely unnoticed. I wanted to understand how he had money to buy so many toys, or how he could make them all alone. Most importantly, I wanted to know who he was, how he lived so long and why he did all that. I had many questions; questions to which, of course, there were no answers. On one occasion, approaching Christmas time, after having interrogated my father for days hoping to get an explanation that was impossible by nature, he strictly forbade me to ask any more questions about Santa Claus. Christmas was coming; Santa Claus existed despite all the contradictions, and that was it. But nothing would stop me from discovering the truth. There would always be next year.

And next year came; December was around the corner and with it came another Christmas. I was then a year older and it was more difficult to dodge my suspicions about Santa Claus with the same old evasive answers. My questions were more scathing, and my parents' strategy now was to try a more feasible Santa Claus adding some surreal elements to the myth. Consequently, what was now more plausible on one hand, on the other hand seemed even more absurd and every answer given only generated more and more questions. Santa Claus' story was unsustainable and the only reason I continued to believe it was because Mom and Dad told me it was all true.

After making my parents exhausted with questions they couldn't answer, my mother decided to come clean. Tactfully and delicately, she explained, according to her own convictions, where Santa Claus' story had come from and why the tradition was perpetuated. As I listened to it all, I felt inevitably relieved. I no longer needed to force myself to believe something that made no sense whatsoever. I would simply not spend any more time with so many questions. They all represented "false problems", as we say in Philosophy. But my mother was truly concerned with the "trauma" this discovery could cause in me. So she did her best in telling me the truth extra carefully.

As minutes and hours passed, my relief turned into inner exuberance. For the first time I felt authorized to accept a truth I long suspected. I was no longer obligated to believe the lie. It was like I was inserted in the adult world, the world of "truth" they insisted to keep hidden from children. However, my mother's expectation was that the "revelation" would make me sad. And in order not to frustrate her, I couldn't let her know the celebration that was taking place inside me. I had to give her a little of what she wanted. Knowing the truth wasn't enough to end the world of appearances.

I've been always surprised by the passivity with which children accept this and other bogus stories. And I've been even more surprised by the almost cynical way in which adults have fun with children's credulity. Clearly, many adults are motivated by affection when they indoctrinate children in these white lies, but it is also true that they enjoy themselves making fun of their kids' ease in believing. It's as if they are reliving their own credulity as children and making fun of themselves for being so naïve.

Adults imagine that children's heads are factories of dreams and fantasies and that, by filling them with old fairy tales, they are only giving them what they need to be children. But a child's mind doesn't manufacture dreams and fantasies, an adult's mind does. Adults are the ones who make romantic fantasies, professional and financial dreams, and ideals of political transformation. Not only they manufacture them, they live intensely immersed in all that searching desperately for meaning in their present lives. A child doesn't need any of that. Children don't need Prince Charming, billionaire professional projects or heroic political revolutions to give them meaning. Children's present lives are already full of meaning; they live here and now. And if a child's here and now seems so much more vivid than the here and now of adults, it's because life is obviously nowhere but here and in no time but now. Children don't need to seek the meaning of life in dreams and fantasies because they are able to grasp it at its source, the source of here and now.

Adults also believe that children will miss the "magic" of Santa Claus in the future if they are deprived of it. But adults are precisely the ones who miss it, they who once believed it! Indeed, every child receives as ideal the world that is first introduced to him. If this world is full of fantasies and lies, children will miss

62

them when they're lost. But if the world they first receive is as realistic and truthful as possible, it will remain after they grow up. Nothing will be lost, and so nothing will be missed. We only miss that which we've lost. There is no possible lack where there are no losses.

Children don't need artificial fantasies in order to be children. They don't need any fantasy at all. Santa Claus exists for adults, not for children. As Middle Age artists depicted children as small adults, adults still imagine that children's minds are imbecile versions of their own. Those who take advantage of children's ingenuity and mock their credulity are up for embarrassing moments once these children enter puberty and start mocking those who used to mock them.

028 – JUDGING IS DIFFERENT FROM CONDEMNING

It's amazing how our day-to-day ethical sense is heavily conditioned by simple and thoughtless assumptions. Among them, the most prominent is perhaps the "judge not lest you be judged". It's one of the most famous passages of the Bible, and it carries the power of Jesus' words. It's generally understood by it that we must try to recognize our own failures of conduct before criticizing that of others. So for as long as we fail we won't be able to criticize the faults of others. As a result, we would live in a world where criticism would be dead.

However, the exhortation to abdicate judgment can't be obeyed. Judging means evaluating, and we never fail to assess the world and people around us under various aspects. Therefore, the exhortation can only actually mean one thing: instead of telling us to stop judging, it tells us to disregard and silence all our judgments. But since it's impossible to stop judging, rather than silencing our judgments we should learn to judge correctly. It turns out that religions deal with the masses, and they can't teach each person how to judge impartially. The only solution is telling them to disregard their own judgments. This is the least damaging alternative.

If each of us could learn to judge correctly, the first lesson would teach us that judging is different from condemning. People don't need to be condemned if our assessment of their conduct is negative. If we can't help judging, we can – and should – avoid condemning others! Even those who are educated and mature still don't understand the difference. They also condemn others when they should simply judge. And worst of all: they condemn those who criticize them, even though the criticism is not condemnatory, appealing to the fact that the critic also has its own flaws. It is not wise to require a critic to be perfect before he can criticize others. This would result in a world without criticism. We all can and should criticize and evaluate other people's conduct, provided we don't condemn them. Critics who refrain from condemning others implicitly include themselves in the crowd they are criticizing. Critics who refrain from condemning know that they're also ordinary people, and that they're also subject to fail in the same way they criticize. Reprehensible are critics who condemn in others what they do. It was against this kind of judgment that Jesus spoke in the Bible. And since then his words have been distorted and used inappropriately to justify intolerance of those who don't accept any kind of criticism. More than that: They were used to justify the hypocrisy and pride of those who attack the flaws of their critics to defend themselves from criticism, although the critics' flaws have nothing to do with the flaws they are criticizing.

No one needs to be perfect in order to be eligible to criticize others. Non-condemning judgment is always positive, even when it disapproves the person being judged. And when disapproval is not condemnatory, it is comforting! When disapproval is exempt from condemnation, the person being judged feels understood. At a minimum, the person being judged feels that the door for dialogue is open, and that makes all his fears smaller. People fear condemnation, not disapproval. It's the fear of being condemned that makes them close in on themselves. That's why people feel comfortable talking to a psychologist about things they can't share with anyone else – even with those who are closest. Psychologists are trained precisely to criticize without condemning. And the fact that our society has turned non-condemning criticism into a profession's specialty is a sad proof of how we are unable to judge each other properly, and of how we condemn each other with the most frivolous and unskilled recklessness.

029 – SOCIAL FOBIA REVEALS THE FARCE OF OUR IDENTITY

Both Psychology and common sense use the term "identity" to refer to our personality without realizing how truthful and proper the term is. Our Self is indeed an identity, but not the identity with ourselves. Our Self establishes its identity with the world. Who are we? We can't answer this question without referencing the world, its objects and other people. We are someone's child, we are the residents of some place, we are the fans of a specific team, and we exercise a particular profession that has its qualities and flaws. A subject is only defined by its objects. That is, in practice, we define our Self by what we have, what we do, our relationships with others, places or situations... we never define our Self for what we are. For indeed the Self is nothing besides all that... The Self is the identity with all that. But if on one hand the Self is the identity with all that, on the other hand it also needs to be different from all that. The Self can't simply be identical to the world. To be in the world and live in it, the Self needs to distinguish itself. Thus, the Self that lives and relates in the world is conscious of being different from it, and its identity with the world remains unconscious.

The unconscious identity of the Self with the world means that the world, and especially those with which the Self relates, exist in the essence of what the Self is. If deep in our souls we are identical to those we relate with, then we can't hide anything from them; we can't keep secrets; we exist in a situation of complete openness and equality with them. In other words, the "gaze of the other" exists within us, and it sees and knows perfectly what we really are. And what is the truth seen by the other's gaze? The gaze of the other sees precisely the difference between us and the world to which we should be identical. Although deep within our souls we are identical to the world, in everyday life we are different from it, and

65

the other's gaze in us clearly sees that! Therefore, our life in the world is an effort (conscious or unconscious) to fool the other's gaze within us and send out to the real others outside us an image similar to their own; we want to make them think we think like them, we like the same things as them; we are part of the same tribes they are. Even when we rebel, we're also acting in this farce. Teenagers only rebel after failing repeatedly in their attempts to fake their identity with the world. And they see rebelling as a way to change the world and make the simulation of identity with it a little easier.

If you allow me to exaggerate a little, I will say that our life is a great play. We live trying to send out to the world an image that differs from what we are. Things go right if we believe that by fooling real people's gaze we are fooling the other's gaze that exists within us. However, when the other's gaze within us is reflected in the eyes of others who are before us, we can't fake the embarrassment. The most typical situation is speaking in public. Faced with the overwhelming presence of tens and even hundreds of exterior eyes, the other's gaze within us also becomes an overwhelming presence in us and breaks our facade! Sometimes the presence of a single person is enough. And even the absence of any real person can suffice for the other's gaze within us to become more real than the real absence outside!

When the other's gaze within resists our attempts to deceive it, we feel like we're being caught red-handed. We no longer know how to behave, we can't react, we freeze. Our farce is threatened. However, this farce is exactly what we are, and the threat to the farce is a threat to our very Self. There are those who experience only a mild embarrassment, and even make fun of it. But there are those who experience large doses of anxiety or even panic. And all because we take the farce seriously. If our Self is a farce, the best option is to recognize it and accept it as a farce. It is precisely our effort to legitimize the farce, which makes us easy prey to the critical gaze of the other within us.

The holiday season arrives and brings along our best wishes for a good New Year. On New Year's Eve, we renew our hope of a better life. We celebrate hope as something positive. If we didn't live on hope, and if we couldn't always refresh it, would we be able to find meaning in life? Or would we drown in anguish?

Hope is the belief in a future positive possibility. However, if the future is only a possibility, it may never occur. Whereas hope is based on the possibility of a future that takes place, fear is based on the opposite possibility. Therefore, where there is hope there is also fear, since both possibilities coexist. Inversely, where there is fear there is hope.

We only fear the evil that hasn't yet happened, the evil that is only a possibility. The evil that is already present doesn't cause fear, only sadness. And if we don't see the possibility of remediation, sadness turns into anguish. If we can't accept anguish as a sign that the evil is irreparable, we are possessed by the urge to repair it at all costs, and anguish turns into anxiety, which can lead to despair or panic.

Hope and fear are two consequences of desire. Desire is the result of present deficiencies, which induce us to expect future satisfaction and to fear it will not occur. And where there is hope and fear there is anguish. Anguish increases over the years with maturity and with the awareness that we are doomed to not finding the profound fulfillment desired, even in spite of the great pleasures and joys that we possibly experienced along the way. The conscious anguish of not having a solution for our greatest needs induces us to hope for a future in which all is resolved. But because this future is only a possibility, it never pulls apart from the distressing reality it wished to break free from. Therefore, hope is full of anguish and anguish is full of hope. And if the meaning of life is lost in anguish, the meaning sought in hope is a fraud, since it is drenched in anguish.

We thoughtlessly celebrate hope as if it were life at its fullest. But in hope, life is as empty as anguish. Hope and anguish are two variations of the same theme. That's why all hope is vain. We

67

celebrate hope as life's most sublime aspect because we know nothing better. Despite our joys, we only find the meaning of life in the emptiness that is hope. We're not aware of how unhappy we are. And we never really think about it. We chase after our dreams, numbing our minds with them in order to escape the anguish that haunts us. And even when our dreams are fulfilled, we still live in the emptiness of hope, ultimately the hope of an afterlife. We must think about this. We must ask ourselves about happiness, what it is and if it's possible. We can be sure that happiness is not the hope we celebrate every holiday. What is it, then? I leave that question wishing that, on the next holiday season, we can be more aware of what happiness is and more prepared to achieve it.

31 – ROMANTIC LOVE IS THE RESIDUE OF LIFE

In our culture, love is confused with romantic love. There is love between friends, family and even between people and animals, but when we talk about love, we generally understand romantic love. The realization of romantic fantasies is high on the priority list of the majority of young adults – and even people in old age. However, an analysis of romantic needs can show that love relationships are based on cues or residues of all other relationships.

When youngsters enter their preteen years, they understand that the distance between them and their parents is greater than they imagined. Children who were once accepted, understood, and protected become lonely preteens. They, who once believed mutual belonging prevailed in the relationship with their parents, now realize there's no ownership over each other. They want to claim ownership of those they love and establish a relationship of unlimited intimacy, security and loyalty, but consider this expectation inappropriate for their present age. Even physical proximity must now comply with age restrictions. In social life, they also learn that it is more convenient to ignore some disappointments and let go of a number of things, as if nothing had happened, to preserve friendships. How nice would it be if we could have, in the beginning of pre-adolescence, a relationship of infinite care, protection, and understanding? A relationship without barriers, including physical barriers, with full access to the physical intimacy of our partner; how nice would it be if we could claim ownership of those we love with no shame and surrender to them on reciprocity? How nice would it be to be able to expose and discuss all the little disappointments and discomfort, with traces of sulky childishness and selfishness? It would be great, too good to be true. Such relationships do not exist, but nothing prevents us from dreaming about them. They're our romantic fantasies, aroused in the moment of realization that real relationships are not what we'd imagined. No loving relationship fulfills such fantasies, but that doesn't stop us from expecting it from our partners.

Romantic fantasies are made of unmet needs in other relationships; they are the set of residues left by them. However, one type of relationship can't compensate for the deficiencies of other relationships. Processing residues of all relationships into one type of relationship generates even more residue. However, if romance is a product of the residual deficiency of adulthood, processing these deficiencies defines this kind of love. That is why romantic relationships are so complicated. They are at the same time the most difficult, the most frustrating, and also the lightest and most satisfactory ones. All that is banned in other relationships, as we grow older, is allowed in romantic relationships. The often austere, distant, and mature formality that characterizes adult relationships can undress itself so we can return to being the obstinate, possessive and needy children we never ceased to be. Nothing is as sublimely pathetic as romanticism.

32 – ANXIETY, DEPRESSION AND THE FANTASY OF AN INVISIBLE FUSE

Anxiety and depression are people's major psychological problems nowadays. Many argue that day-to-day stress is primarily responsible for anxiety and that depression is caused mainly by the lack of meaning of a materialistic life. But why should the daily life rush make us anxious? And why would a materialistic life be meaningless? The rush and materialism impose goals for us to achieve. We buy romantic, professional, financial and personal dreams. We look around and see others also buying and surrendering to the same dreams. The normality standard rose well above normal. The current normal standard demands perfection. One must have the perfect body, the perfect love partner, the perfect profession, the stuffed bank account and a social life full of parties and best friends.

The goals of today's world are now the normality standard because they have become common to the point that we can no longer imagine life without them. For us, there is only life in the achievement of these goals, and not complying with them makes life unfeasible. Thus, it is easy to understand why there is so much anxiety today: in our imagination, we constantly strive against death. Even a simple Friday night out acquires dramatic tones. "Everyone goes out on Friday night. Staying at home is not normal! It's worse than death!" But when the struggle for perfection doesn't result in the expected happiness, or when its standards seem unattainable to us, we enter a dead end. If we can't imagine life beyond unattainable goals, our impulse to live becomes depressed.

Today's goals are our inner, invisible fuse. We believe that not complying with those goals would cause the fuse to burn and life to cease. But the invisible fuse doesn't exist. It represents arbitrary limits below which we imagine that life would become unbearable. However, when any of these limits is exceeded we certainly suffer, but we learn that life goes on. The fantasy of the invisible fuse is a consolation, in a way. It is comforting to believe that things can't be too bad, and that there's a bearable limit to suffering, beyond which there's nothing left, neither pain nor pleasure. To undo the fantasy of an invisible fuse is to understand that we can withstand anything, and that can make us desperate. This despair is not anxiety, but resignation; because undoing the fantasy of an invisible fuse is to understand that life doesn't depend on our usual goals. Thus, the whole rush to compliance loses the power to make us anxious and to delude us as to the meaning they can give to life. Those who can undo the fantasy of the invisible fuse to the bottom of their soul become immune to anxiety and depression. This doesn't necessarily bring happiness, but it certainly puts them in with anguish before it turns into anxiety or depression. If everyone became aware that the limits of a bearable life are arbitrary and imaginary, the industry of antidepressants and other anxiolytics would go bankrupt.

33 – MOTIVATION: THE DRUG OF THIS CENTURY

The number of professionals specialized in motivational processes is on the rise. HR consultants are essential to keep company employees motivated. And why do employees need motivation? For executing a job that doesn't fulfill them and being paid a salary that doesn't satisfy them. Even those who get paid well need motivation. A low income is not always the problem. When work doesn't fulfill us, we seek motivation in the payment. But what if the payment, though generous, doesn't satisfy? In that case, it takes even more motivation. Motivational professionals are experts in producing it to convince us there's value in the grueling work in which we vainly seek sense.

The possibility of getting married revives a dating relationship that has gone bad. When the marriage is bad, it is the desire to have children that strengthens it. In order to overcome the difficulties of raising our children, we rely on the illusion to establish with them an idealized relationship never before held; that illusion ends when our children grow up and our relationship with them has its difficulties. The promise of marriage motivates us to continue ignoring the problems of a bad dating relationship. Having children motivates us to escape from the reality of a marriage that doesn't work. The illusion of an ideal relationship is the motivation that always leads us to seek in others the intimacy that we don't have with our own Self. And professional life goals motivate us to believe that there's sense in sacrificing life because of excessive work. The motivation of the dating relationship is not in the dating itself, because it is bad. The same goes for marriage, the children and work. The love relationship is unsatisfactory, raising children is a burden and work replaces life. However, we live enthusiastically and with motivation. And a motivated person is easily confused with a happy person! For what other definition is there for happiness? We believe that the most motivated people are the happiest, those whose life has most meaning. In the common sense, motivation is the secret of living well. It is so important that if you could make it into pills, all our problems would be solved! And isn't that the great promise of antidepressants?

When family, love and work relationships are unsatisfactory, which motivation can compensate for them? And what when one doesn't have a family, a home, a job, a future? Which motivation can help overcome all that? Can we run away from violence and destruction? Is there any motivation that can compensate a whole life left aside and help us avoid our own destructiveness?

If motivated people are happy, why are they so anxious? Why can't they find peace? If they are fulfilled, why do they need so much confusion and outside commotion? Why can't they be alone with themselves, enjoying the abundance that exists inside them? Why do they drink, smoke, and engage in sufferable relationships? What do they seek other than the destruction of the life they claim to love? If motivated people knew how to live, would they need so much motivation? Why do we need motivation to aid life? Why don't we live now? Don't we have life here and now, in our very hands? Why don't we just live? Too many questions, not a single answer.

34 – SELFISHNESS IS NOT A CLASS PRIVILEGE

Our Self is formed by identification, which is paradoxical. As identification progresses, it increases the awareness of our identity with the world because we take a country as nationality, we learn its language, we acquire values, we begin using a family name, etc. However, with the progress of identification, the awareness of differences between the world and us also rises, because it's through identification that, while acquiring an individualized consciousness of a Self, we take on the condition of individuals. Therefore, the well-formed Self, reaching its identity with the world, establishes the identity with itself and the awareness of its individuality. However, the absolute identity with oneself is an abstraction. The Self doesn't consume its identity. So, the Self defines its identity through the reference to its worldly relationships, or by possession: my body, my family, my country, my values, my knowledge, my things, etc. The relationship between the Self and the world, intermediated by the possessiveness expressed in this "my", is selfishness.

Possessiveness is made of desire. In a non-consummated identity, one lacks fulfillment, and desire gives worldly relations the purpose of finding that which will fulfill us. However, we lack an identity with our Self, and no mundane object will fit perfectly where that identity is missing. But desires can be satisfied, although satisfaction does not fulfill us. Soon after the satisfaction, desire returns forcing us to seek for more of it. The momentary satisfaction leads us to believe that fulfillment will be reached in some form of intense satisfaction. Thus, we don't abandon our possessiveness: on the contrary, we learn to possess more and in a better way, never accepting affective and material conditions lower than those to which we have become accustomed. If affective or sensual relations are what satisfies us, we will seek more affection and more sex. If what satisfies us is power and professional success, there'll be no limits! If what flatters us is knowledge, we'll live surrounded by books. And if possessions are what polishes our Self, winning and losing money will be an endless game.

It's not hard to imagine that a world of selfish people is cruel, violent and marked by a gap between the rich and the poor. But we haven't yet understood that selfishness exists in all, regardless of social class. Of course, the rich and powerful also have more responsibilities and owe more explanation. However, this doesn't justify society's naïve division into those who are guilty and the victims. The humblest usually cling less to material things, as they have learned to live without them. However, their selfishness works in other domains, such as the affective, and would also be conditioned to the satisfaction of luxury as soon as it became usual. Habit conditions us to always want more of what that which has become common. That's a psychological premise, not a class privilege. Sociology and the most progressive economies need to take hold of this psychology, understand it and develop it if they are to contribute to a better society. Theories that fight the difference between classes give way to revanchism between the rich and the poor, employees and employers. They only analyze material relations when they should examine and understand human relationships. When human relationships come into debate, we will finally be able to elucidate the responsibility of each one of us and stop conveniently blaming a minority for a world that belongs to all.

35 – WHY DO WE FEEL DISTANT FROM THOSE WE LOVE THE MOST?

At birth, we are confronted with a world of natural and interpersonal obstacles. Growing up and developing oneself means adapting to the world. In the process, we build an image of the world. At the same time, we build an image of ourselves which we consider suits best the demands of the world. Living and having relationships is to strive to pass on the image of being adapted to world. But it also means to demand from the world that it should fit the image we built in the first place. When the world surprises us, it triggers the mismatch between itself and its image. However, we also find ourselves sometimes with the realization that our self-image, so far well adapted, disagrees with what we are.

We do not relate directly with our Self or with the world, but with our self-image and the image of the world, which are ideals of what we and the world should be to us. Our self-image imposes on us the obligation of adapting to the demands of the world as if they came from the world itself. And our image of the world forces it to adapt to our demands as if there was a natural obligation. In addition to obligating ourselves to the world, we also oblige it to us, and this two-way street is especially true for human relationships. The closest family relationships are among the most idealized. The relationship between parents and children, for example, is mediated by the roles of parents and children, which adapt to each other while children are young and disagree as soon as they grow a little. When parents and children realize the inadequacy of the relationship, they tend to blame each other. Children complain that their parents treat them like children, and parents complain that their children don't behave like adults. However, children don't want to stop receiving paternal treatment, and parents don't want to not have them as their babies. Both sides feel trapped by the each other's demands. Nevertheless, the demands on one side are the counterpart of the other side's demands. If the children did not demand that parents be parents, they wouldn't feel imprisoned by the role of children, and vice versa.

Thus, the affection nourished between parents and children doesn't translate into the proximity and intimacy that it should theoretically condition, and the same goes for any idealized relationship, such as love. When we feel trapped by someone else to a role that's inadequate to who we are and when we demand from others that they fit a role unsuitable to who they are, intimacy or closeness cannot happen. The chagrin of love not lived is all that remains.

36 – REJECTION IS NOT THE END OF THE WORLD

Loneliness, death, and rejection are our greatest fears. On social networks, we can observe how rejection bothers people and how they can't handle it. Feeling rejected, people run for self-affirmation and write posts such as "I'm the best", "I don't care about what others think," etc. All a facade. Deep inside, these people are the ones who care the most about other people's opinion and suffer the most when rejected.

Relationships with others are directly linked to the relationship with one's Self, and vice versa. Therefore, those who have good relationships also have a good relationship with their Self. Thus one who can relate well with others can also be alone. And by the fear people share of loneliness, we can assess that they don't know how to relate with themselves, nor, consequently, with others. The difficulty in the relationship with others is linked to the need for acceptance. We want the ideal person that will accept us as we are. In the absence of acceptance, we feel rejected. In the search for acceptance, we sell to others what we think is the best image of ourselves. We sell that image because, in general, we build an image of others and we believe that it demands, as a counterpart, the image we sell of ourselves. Thus, rejection is understood as a breach of contract, because we believed that our image must be accepted. And if others refuse to accept that image, we conclude they weren't worthy of the affection we invested in trying to make them accept it. Therefore, after rejection comes hurt, and along with hurt comes the self-affirmation attitude.

Why does the need for acceptance upset our relationships that much? Because it brings the demands that we make to others. The image we build of others summarizes all that we think they should be, do, or think. By demanding them to accept us as we are, we demand others to be, do, or think as we consider right. Not only we demand that others accept us as we are; we also demand that they fit into our standards so we accept them as they are. When we suffer a rejection or when we imagine we're being rejected, we question our adequacy. "Is there something wrong with me?", we think. We never think we're being rejected because people feel inadequate to the image we have of them; that is, they also feel inadequate to the demands that we make to them and unable to answer in the way we expected.

Reviewing the demands we make to others means reviewing the image of ourselves that we pass on to them and investigating our need for acceptance. In other words, the fewer demands we make to others, the less we expect them to fit our predetermined patterns, the less we will need to feel accepted by them. And the lower the need for acceptance, the less likely we are to feel rejected and the greater our tolerance to loneliness.

The Self is constituted in the paradoxical process that makes it increasingly aware of its identity with people while making it more aware of its individual and independent existence. The Self, conscious of its own identity with others, is aware of its identity with itself, and therefore, it is aware of being a person different from all others. Both the awareness of identity and the awareness of its difference from others are based on the identification with the people around. For this reason, a weird look can shake our identity. If the identificatory bond with others suffers a setback, our identity is destabilized; it's like the safety of what we are would come to weaken.

When others see us as strange, we feel strange. Our identity depends on a steady understanding between the Self and others. We must recognize in people what we are and what they are, as they should recognize in us what they are and what we are so that the awareness of our identity is preserved. So if the habit of receiving disapproval and criticism conditions us to a negative self-image, others should recognize this image in us so that our identity is preserved. Thus, without noticing, we will give them what they expect to receive – or that which we need to give them: a negative image of ourselves. We will hide feelings, words, and actions that could give them a positive image of us only because we're afraid they'll see us as weird. Those used to being seen as bad are perceived as strange – or feel strange – when showing their good side. Suddenly, others no longer know how to react to them and they don't know how to react to people either. To avoid this embarrassment, these people may become worse than they are only because they know what is expected of them, something common among children who are often criticized and disapproved. Of course, the opposite also occurs: If the habit of being complimented conditions a positive self-image, we will probably pass on to others a picture of us that is better than what we really are by burying words, feelings, actions, and opinions that could reveal our worst side.

Those who strive to pass on to others a worse image of themselves and those who strive to pass on a better image both believe they are conveying an image of what they are. The desire to pass on to others the image they expect to receive from us conditions our Self's unconsciousness. Showing a worsened image of oneself is to suffer for the guilt of not being as good as he should be without knowing he is already better than he'd like to be. Showing an enhanced image of oneself is to rejoice for never having been worse without allowing the consciousness of being this worse. And our self-image not always adjusts with time. So it is important to analyze criticisms and expectations thrown at us in order to separate the wheat from the chaff and form a realistic picture of what we are. Within each one of us there's an ugly duckling that hasn't become a swan and a common duck who thinks he's become one. Like Freud once said, "We would be much better people if we didn't want to be so good."

38 – WE CAN'T ALWAYS "DO SOMETHING"

The feeling of omnipotence the contemporary man has reveals itself in the unconscious fantasy about ubiquitous human agents. We say that "they" will solve it, "they" know everything, "they" are to blame. "They" are the agents of all good and bad things. "They" are everywhere. "They" are the contemporary version of God. But whereas God is a non-human entity, "they" are among us and walk with human legs, even though we don't know who they are. We only experience the beneficial or harmful effects of their alleged actions; effects that are everywhere and affect our lives completely. So although we're aware "they" are human, we unconsciously believe in their ubiquity. The term "they" is the humanization of omnipotence. And if "they" are human and can do anything, so can we.

The fantasy of "them" presents two seemingly opposite effects. On the one hand, it encourages the common person's passivity before collective problems. No one does anything, no one goes anywhere because we trust that "they" will do something and fix everything. Not even the constant experience of not having "them" solving anything undoes the belief in "them". Similarly, the belief in God remains constant even with the constant experience of not having "him" solving anything. On the other hand, the belief in "them" encourages the ideal of activity, autonomy, and self-sufficiency in the common person, and it fosters the belief that there is always something to do to solve a problem. Many believe that the only thing to which there's no solution is death; for everything else, there's always an alternative. However, this ideal leads to anxiety before what can't be changed.

There is only one form of autonomy in the face of what can't be changed: Resignation. In the absence of resignation, we imprison ourselves in the anxious dependence of the desire to change what is out of reach. Eventually, this anxiety knocks us out and leads us to depression, baring the impotence of the lack of resignation. Resignation keeps us free before restrictions that we cannot topple. So, amid people who are anxious and certain of their own omnipotence, resignation is understood as conformism. However, the distinction between what can be changed and what cannot works only in resignation.

It's hard to accept whatever bothers us in others as something that's not likely to change. It is hard to accept other people's choices as not amendable. It's even harder to understand that it is necessary to accept whatever bothers us in ourselves so that change may occur, and that acceptance is already the desired change. Our focus of anxiety is the tension between what we believe we are and what we believe we should be. The understanding that we're already what we want to be lies only in resignation.

We can't be responsible for everything. And those who believe they can always do something, never knowing what exactly, will ask someone to tell them what to do or how to something they don't even know. It's the illusion of autonomy revealed in the greatest passivity of all: the passivity that's not autonomous even to admit itself as passive.

Loneliness is not only the lack of company, but the need to see our tastes, our opinions, our desires mirrored in others. More profoundly, it is the need to see our fears and anxieties understood by others, divided and shared with them. In the absence of being in contact with oneself, loneliness is, ultimately, the desire to mediate this contact through others. We seek with others the intimacy that we don't have with our Self without realizing that it can't be found there. So loneliness presents a dilemma: we lack intimacy with our Self, but don't know how to find it in us; we know how to look for it with others, but it is not there to be found.

The more superficial the intimacy of the Self with itself, the more superficial the intimacy sought with others will be. That is why so many surrender to the noise and uproar of the crowd. In the case of elderly people, they are commonly not able to go beyond the "small talk". Superficial intimacy has an advantage: it can be easily found. It is relatively easy to find company for fun times, but the relief it provides is temporary. Those affected by that loneliness need constant company and being alone causes them anxiety.

In turn, the deeper the identity of the Self with itself, the deeper the intimacy sought with others. That is why so many prefer to share memories and confessions. Deep intimacy with others is not easy to find, but its pursuit has the advantage of making people exercise tolerance toward the lack of company. However, if the lack of company is not accompanied by anxiety, social interaction often is.

Those seeking deep intimacy know people's resistance in allowing this contact. And if close contact is not possible, it is preferable not to have any contact whatsoever. Thus, in this pursuit, deep intimacy is only established with few, leaving others with an intimacy that is even more superficial than the intimacy obtained in social life. In this sense, the search for superficial intimacy promotes greater intimacy than the search for deep intimacy.

Those seeking deeper intimacy with others don't know how to find depth in superficiality. The same goes, in a different sense, for those seeking superficial intimacy. So both searches expose the lack of contact with one's Self, and those eager to be alone are as lonely as those eager for social life. The loneliness of those who are extroverted and introverted are two sides of the same coin, and a proof of that is the loneliness that summarizes both and to which all are subject: the lack of a loving partner. Those seeking a loving partner seek company, someone to shoot the breeze with, and someone to share memories and confessions and to make them feel understood. In the absence of love, people seek deep contact in the superficiality of romantic idealization. It masks the search for deep intimacy giving it the lightness of a fantasy novel; and it masks the pursuit of superficial intimacy giving it the aura of a deep desire to be close to a loved one. Romanticism is the opium of loneliness; it makes loneliness numb and prevents us from knowing it better.

40 – PSYCHIATRIC DIAGNOSES EXPLAIN NOTHING

Psychiatric diagnoses are fashionable these days. Suddenly, everyone is depressed, bipolar, has panic disorder or another type of anxiety disorder. Surely, these diagnoses are part of the psychology of everyday life. However, we do not stop to think what they mean and what actually explain.

The depression diagnosis is given when the behavior fits the diagnostic lines of depression. And the same goes for all psychiatric diagnoses. Therefore, the diagnosis only classifies behavior as depressed without giving any explanation. Depression is nothing but behavior classified as depressed. Therefore, depression cannot explain behavior. Saying that depression explains depressed behavior is to say that depressed behavior explains itself.

Explaining behavior is not the role of psychiatric diagnosis; its role is to provide directions in which behavior should be treated. If a patient is diagnosed with depression, the current treatments for this disorder are likely to have an effect on him. However, we don't need to explain depression – we don't even need to be capable of explaining it – to prescribe treatment. Therapies are developed through trial and error, especially drug therapies. Various drugs are tested until one of them shows the desired effect, but how they work is not always understood. Thus, the role of psychiatric diagnosis is not to explain, but rather to justify the therapy prescribed, usually a drug therapy.

Those who don't act within the standards may suffer quite a lot with being misunderstood by others and by themselves, until they are given a psychiatric diagnosis. Then, everything is suddenly clear: "He is like that because he's depressed", "She is like that because she's borderline", etc. It's as if people believed that depression or borderline disorder are a "thing", a foreign body within the patient that causes their behavior and justifies it.

Depression is not a foreign body inside the patient and it isn't the cause of anything. People become depressed because of their choices, their own way of seeing the world and acting on it. And if their family did not understand that before the diagnosis, the diagnosis isn't what will make them understand. In this case, it will only serve to label the person as sick and remove him from the "normal" group; it will only serve, in short, to make others treat him differently. And patients enjoy this situation. For if the diagnosis justifies their behavior in the eyes of others, it may serve to justify him to himself. From that point on, everything can be a consequence of depression, panic disorder, borderline disorder, etc.

We must stop trying to understand ourselves and others through psychiatric diagnoses. It is the most superficial of the popular psychologies. People must be understood in the context of their life, their way of thinking and of how the world reacted to them. Only this understanding can help rescue them from the passivity of the patient condition (or worse: the medicated patient condition) and make them agents of their own lives.

82

The habit of explaining personality by genetic inheritance is part of tradition. In simple language we say, for example, that the son "took after" a parent in a given personality trait. From the second half of the twentieth century on, this habit gained a scientific aura because science started identifying genetic inheritance as the cause of similarities in the personalities of blood-related people.

Genetic heredity explains physical and psychological similarities between people of the same family. It had already been noticed for some time, and now it has an explanation: Parents pass their genes onto their children, and two people genetically similar may have similar personalities. However, if on one hand, heredity explains why the personality of relatives may be alike, on the other hand it does not provide any explanation for why we are as we are.

The genetic code determines the way we initially react to the world. The way we react to the world is what we call personality. Even though the genetic code determines the initial way in which we react to the world, it does not change throughout life. However, among the traits determined by it, the ability to change our personality is indelibly there. So we see ourselves as free or endowed with free will. And if we can change our personality without changing the genetic code, the code isn't the cause of personality. The causes for our personality are in it, and so it is changeable. If its causes were external, as an unalterable and passively inherited genetic code, we would be unable to change ourselves.

The origin of character is not in recent genetic inheritance or phylogenetic inheritance. The Evolution Theory explains how and why certain genes have been passed on from generation to generation for thousands of years until today. But our personality wasn't originated thousands of years ago. It begins when we are born, and it can be developed and matured. Personality develops each time we understand the motivation of our behavior; and it matures every time we use this understanding to modify ourselves toward adaptation. A mature personality is one that has learned to know itself in order to adapt. In the adaptation process, it investigates its own motivations. Therefore, the cause for personality is its own motivations. To explain it, one must find out the reasons – yet hidden – for personality and analytically reconstruct the path that brought it into its present form. Each person's motivations are personal, never inherited. Therefore, it makes no sense to explain personality by any kind of inheritance.

42 – WHAT IS THE DIFFERENCE BETWEEN MORALISM AND MORALITY?

Nowadays, old values are questioned and taken down. We live a transition in which the letting go of what's old is yet to be accompanied by what's new. We live in a plurality of value systems. And if multiplicity is valid, there is no absolute truth. Everything is relative, there is a shortage of references and traditional values are labeled as moralists. The battle against moralism is in fashion, but only a few know how to define moralism and distinguish it from morality.

Any old, conservative ethical principle that restricts social and sexual behavior is understood as moralistic. However, this definition is not accurate. There is no such thing as a moralistic ethical principle. Moralism refers to how an ethical principle is justified. Moralistic ethical principles are justified by authority, be it tradition authority, authority of those who raised us, or religion authority. In turn, morality considers what is best for the individual and for the society. Thus, the same ethical principle can be defended in a moral or moralistic way by changing the argument assumptions. The moral defense will argue that obedience to the principle is beneficial to the individual and society, and will see disobedience as harmful, while the moralist defense will argue that its validity is based on any given form of authority.

Old ethical principles seem moralist because their defense uses traditionally moralistic arguments. An ethical principle defended in a moralistic way does not involve discussion because authority must be indisputable in order to be valid. Morality, in turn,

84

supports debate. Debate is endless, by the way, in the field of morality – and it should be so. Morality is concerned with what is best for the individual and society, not with blind obedience to values imposed by authority, and the discussion around what is best for us has no end.

Even a conservative ethical principle should be analyzed and considered if its defense shows benefits in case of obedience and harm in case of disobedience. The conservatism and seniority of a principle does not make it automatically odious. It is also possible to learn how to make today's world a better place with old values. Morality, on the other hand, hinders this learning by holding us to automatically following rules without debate. Therefore, moralistic arguments should be excluded not only from our personal lives, but also – and mainly – the public sphere.

It is not relevant to ask how will end the process of ethical restructuring we are living. It is more important to ensure it is mediated by the debate, not by moralistic constraints.

43 – LOVE IS NOT AN OBLIGATION

Love is usually treated as an obligation, which creates conflicts. The girl thinks her boyfriend is wonderful. The boy is attentive and helpful; he is everything a woman expects in a man. But she does not love him; not the way she should love a boyfriend, and this makes her suffer. She tries to convince herself otherwise, and is torn by doubt. She doesn't know if she likes him or not. In fact, she would know she doesn't like him if she didn't feel obligated to. She fell for the ideal man image and deceived herself not realizing she doesn't necessarily feel attracted by it. Beauty isn't always attractive, ugliness isn't always repulsive. We don't always love the beautiful and hate the ugly. The girl who builds romantic fantasies in the existing molds may feel obliged to love those who fit in them without realizing she wants something quite different.

Being involved with non-ideal types can also bring a similar feeling of obligation. A girl might, for instance, have a boyfriend who's deeply cherished by her mother and friends and she might feel guilty for not feeling the same. Does she have a problem? Why can't she see all the qualities in her boyfriend that others see? It's not that she fails to see it; those who look from a distance believe to have a better view than whoever looks closely. They are the only ones who see up close and really know their loving partners. Still, they don't seem to be prepared to support their point of view when everybody thinks differently. So, they believe they have a special love partner who deserves to be loved.

Even if the loving partner is special, affinity might be lacking, and love is a matter of affinity. We shouldn't love only those who are beautiful and special; we should love those with whom we have affinity. And love happens spontaneously, without obligation. Many seek a psychologist's help with doubts about their feelings for their loving partners. If there's doubt, the answer might be negative, since doubt indicates the sense of obligation; the feeling of having a gratitude debt to be paid in the love currency. Love is not a bargaining currency. We either love or don't. When there's doubt about whether love is present, it might not be present in the form expected, that is, romance. Doubt will possibly reveal other ways to love that are different from the appropriate way of loving a loving partner.

But there are also cases where doubt is a sign of the conflict between authentic feelings and the immaturity of our fantasies. We idealize the ideal partner and we frustrate ourselves with the reality of a loving relationship, not realizing that we are connected to our partner through bonds that, though deep, do not fit in the romantic idealization. Thus, the doubt reveals the need to mature our fantasies and embrace reality.

Cases where the obligation makes love seem larger than it is are worse. Wherever there is a sense of obligation, there lies duty; and wherever there is a breach of duty, there lies the guilt feeling. Whenever guilt is not well elaborated, compensation arises. Compensation for those who believe they love less than they should is to love more than they could; it is to erase oneself in love. Those who disappear in love may do it gladly when in love, or by sacrifice if there is no passion. When sacrifice is the outcome of passion, the case is less serious. For Passion is temporary, and eventually an opportunity comes that makes it possible to build a mature relationship. However, when sacrifice exists with no passion, it is a compensation for the guilt feeling, and compensation of guilt produce the strange effect of requiring more and more compensation, sinking us deeper and deeper in the dependency on a self-destructive relationship.

44 – CAN ONLY DEATH TEACH US HOW TO LIVE?

Collective tragedies awaken in the public an empathy for the suffering of others in such a way that we don't see every day. Suddenly, your suffering is mine, my suffering is yours, I am unable to continue pretending I don't suffer, you feel unable to continue pretending you don't suffer, and both you and I have no choice but to look at each other and recognize the same pain that is mine and yours. When so many are unexpectedly affected by death, the curtains of the show of life rise and the reality is imposed on everyone. And if on one hand reality is hard enough for them to feel the sharp end of play being staged, on the other hand it brings the warmth lacking in the acting performance.

Although we live the unconscious fantasy of immortality, we never stop fearing death, but not exactly physical death. The fantasy of immortality is about the body. The death that threatens us is psychological. We believe that we will be sucked into the black abyss of anguish, if we let our minds cool down. One must keep it always high. Any taint is a threat. We neglect the suffering and indefinitely postpone its confrontation. After all, we are immortal! The final judgement day may be postponed! Then, suddenly death occurs. The fantasy of immortality is defeated by the reality that forces us to face what has been overlooked.

Those who neglect their own pain neglect the pain of others as well. We neglect the pain of others with indifference, destructive criticism, or futile advice that keeps us apart. Thus, in death we suffer not only for the loss, but for everything we never lived with whoever is now gone, because we were busy neglecting both our pain and theirs. We prefer to give in to drinking, smoking, to the easy laugh, to ideologies, religions and abstract philosophies, frivolous companies and amusements than having seen them without restrictions and allowing them to mirror ourselves. If we had been at their side, perhaps the pain of loss were less. But death brings this look of mutual recognition, precisely this ever feared look, and we discover there's no threat. We felt threatened by not experiencing that look. Our need of it was so intense that we feared getting lost in if we allowed ourselves to exchange it with someone. So, we understand that there is no need for us to live life as a theatre play, and that we are better on the hard ground of reality than acting. Why don't we live each day in the same empathy?

We're better in death than in life. It is in death that we discover how good we could be or could have been. Why aren't we as good in life as we are in death? Why do we have so much fear that it makes us live for the ideologies, beliefs and vain amusements if it's on the hard ground of reality that we finally find what we need? Is only death able to teach us how to live?

45 – WE MUST ABANDON THE PAST IN ORDER TO FIND IT AGAIN

In the age of computers and information, evolution and development are understood in a linear, ascending and quantitative way. The latest computer is better than the previous for having more memory and processing speed. However, the development of personality cannot be analyzed that way. The difference between a child and an adult is not only a matter of better or worse settings. Not everything that is acquired to become an adult is better than what is lost when one is no longer a child. In the process of growing and maturing, all gain comes accompanied by loss in another sense, and whatever is lost along the way often creates significant gaps. Something essential for happiness in mature age is left behind, and the process of becoming mature may consist of repeated efforts to reintegrate in the present that which has already been lost.

The need to reintegrate in the present what has been lost is real. The development that leads to happiness in mature age needs the reintegration in the present of what has been lost in the past. However, this need can delude us making us believe that happiness is a kind of reliving what happened. This is the negative aspect of nostalgia. For the past is gone, it cannot be re-edited, and the desire to relive it only results in frustration. We live in the expectation of the past being found again in the future. Thus, the present is no longer lived, and frustration is the consequence of what we don't live here and now.

Reintegrating the past into the present, something so essential for happiness, requires us to abandon the past in a sense and rediscover it in another. It requires that the past be transformed and assimilated as something new. Only a renewed past can become present, because the present is always unprecedented. The ideals of professional success, social transformation and romantic relationship built in adulthood have both the germ of renewal and the fixation in the past. Problems arise when we try to revive the past that was lost in achieving the ideals. Those seeking to relive in romantic fantasies the ideal relationship status between the child and their parents, or those who seek to relive the condition of equality between brothers ruled by paternalistic instances in the realization of social projects will inevitably fall into contradiction. In their actions, a quest for the restitution of a childish condition will be clear rather than the effort to establish new patterns of relationship or society.

There is wisdom in nostalgia. On one hand, it preserves the memory of something that is still essential. On the other, it forces us to recognize that this essential has been lost. Recalling fills the present with hopes to finding it again, but it also forces us to accept that it is not possible to find it again in the form already lived. The past must be abandoned so it can be rediscovered.

046 – THERE IS NO LIFE WITHOUT DISCRIMINATION

Discrimination and prejudice are open wounds in our days. In a society where people are harmed by their skin color, gender, sexuality and physical disabilities, it is expected that the beginning of the struggle for equality awaken exaggeratedly hard feelings. Therefore, we must be careful not to go out "on a witch-hunt". To learn is to acquire preconceptions. Abandoning our preconceptions means leaving aside everything we've learned so far and starting over. Preconceptions are previously acquired concepts, which help us make decisions. Every decision implies discrimination. Without discrimination, there would be no choice, not even the simple choice of getting out of bed in the morning.

Discrimination and preconceptions are essential for social welfare. If we had not acquired preconceptions about children and we didn't use them to discriminate children from adults, we wouldn't be able to protect children from whatever's inappropriate for them. When our preconceptions provide an adequate ground to our discrimination, we act wisely. Trouble arises when we discriminate based on inadequate preconceptions – prejudice, that is. However, although most color, gender, sexuality and physical disabilities discrimination is wrong, there are exceptions. At a job interview, dismissing a black applicant for a job that can be done by anyone regardless of his skin color is unjustified discrimination. On the other hand, if an actor is being cast to play Superman on the big screen, a black actor probably won't be chosen, since the character in the comic book is white. The competence of black actors who want to play the role will not matter much. Unless an alternate version of Superman is produced, black actors will not be casted. Similarly, white, blue-eyed actors would hardly be chosen to play Martin Luther King, unless we consider a free narrative of this historical figure.

These are examples of justifiable skin color discrimination. The preconception that grounds them is adequate, and there would be no reason for resentment if society was formed of mature individuals. But the reactions to discrimination acts such as these show that we haven't yet achieved such maturity. Exaggerated sensitivity to similar discrimination acts serves to attack the unjust discrimination as well as the justifiable one. In the example above,

90

if black actors were dismissed at a Superman casting, it is possible that the actors themselves or representatives of organizations against racism would protest because the black actors are as good as the white ones, accusing the producers of prejudice and intolerance. Indeed, the color of an actor's skin doesn't interfere when it comes to being as good as any other; it is also true that society is racist and intolerant. But when truths such as these form the ground for attacks to justified discrimination, injustice is made and we can't fight injustice with more injustice.

Public opinion dislikes just causes when they become witch-hunts and reacts grudgingly where they remain fair. We must be careful with excesses. A little caution never hurt anyone.

47 – THE IMAGINATION THAT HAUNTS THE FUTURE CAN LIVEN UP THE PRESENT

Imagination hunts us ever since childhood. Our own imagination made us fear monsters in the dark, for example. It fills the dark with monsters whose presence children can't really feel. The dark represents the absence of another human being. Therefore, if we only talk to them in the dark, their fears will dissipate. Even being totally alone, a child is often able to control his fear by turning on the light and recognizing the environment. It is then that he begins to understand that being alone is not so terrible, and the monsters are grotesque pictures of his own loneliness. We grow old, and monsters don't abandon us; they disguise themselves. We continue imagining loneliness as a monstrous thing. However, with maturity, we are able to analyze deeper. Instead of interpreting monsters as caricatures of our loneliness, we identify loneliness as the reason for us to fill our lives with monsters.

Loneliness doesn't only mean being alone. Loneliness is the emotional breakup with the world. Wherever there is affective isolation there is loneliness. So one can feel lonely even when standing in the middle of a crowd. If there's no emotional exchange with people around, we will certainly feel alone. And loneliness will most likely be accompanied by imaginary monsters.

People around us will seem ugly to us. We will disapprove of their conversation, we'll consider it trivial and superficial. We will see our own environment as a prison without bars. If we're lucky to have minimally satisfactory interaction with someone along the day, the environmental setting will change entirely. Suddenly, what was once a hopeless prison becomes a space of possibilities – albeit small. If this interaction does not occur, the monsters will haunt us on the way home.

This is a little example of how imagination can haunt us all our lives and even lead us to depression. The great dangers of imagination are on how we anticipate the future and the consequences of that anticipation on our choices. When we're emotionally isolated, fear takes over our imagination of the future. And when fear takes control of the imagination, all possibilities seem fatal. Haunted by a fatalistic future, we judge ourselves powerless. We give up trying to change things and surrender passively to a fate that seems inevitable. Fear leaves us with no choice: danger is imminent, and if you can't solve it completely, you can't solve it at all. And since solving it completely is not a possible solution, the alternative is to give up.

In isolation, fear occupies the space left by affection. And where there is fear there is no life. When we imagine too much and don't live the present, the future seems like a dark place and is difficult to digest. A minimum re-establishment of affective exchange is enough to make us understand that danger isn't so imminent and that it can be solved little by little, if we start from the beginning. We understand that we can breathe and go on living, moving forward one day at a time. The future doesn't have to be resolved immediately, and not all its possibilities are fatal. When fear no longer controls imagination, imagination ceases to haunt the future and starts coloring the present.

48 – WHEN AFFECTION BECOMES DEROGATORY

Laughter is ambiguous. It keeps away that which we want to approach; it expresses our chains and our freedom. In human relations, laughter expresses both depreciation and affection, always at the same time, although we are sometimes more aware of one or the other. As an expression of affection, laughter manifests the wish to approach what is different. As an expression of depreciation, it expresses the wish to ward off what is identical. In short, when there is conflict, laughter solves it, for good or for evil.

In games among adolescents, conflict is visible. Affection displays are aggressive, and displays of explicit aggression are overflowing with the frustrating helplessness of relating to others, who are different – or too similar. Many friendships are established on foundations of jokes and bullying. And even though affection is genuine in these relationships, so is depreciation. So, if a friendship doesn't mature over time, it can become more destructive than constructive.

The derogatory side of affection is not only the explicit laughter. Compassion for vulnerable, troubled people sometimes hides derogatory criticism. Advice used to raise the spirits of those who are down can be outrageous. They despise the intelligence and maturity of a person in need of help. Outrageous, however, is not necessarily the advice content, but rather the attitude of whom advises. They themselves are unable to believe in the value of what they say, and cannot conceal how funny they find their own speech. And whereas voice and body language may conceal well, the looks don't lie. Still, affection is there. At some point, the desire to comfort was authentic, but authenticity went astray in the task of putting themselves in someone else's shoes. Temptation to disparage those who are beneath is greater than the desire to approach them.

There may also be depreciation in the tenderest forms of affection. Those who infantilize babies and children are enchanted by the children's condition that, in his imagination, moves away from his own. Infantilization wants to preserve children in that tender, inferior status. What makes adults delighted with children's attitudes is their unconscious inferiority. A child is spontaneously childish, without knowing he is a child. Better yet: They act as if they knew and didn't care, didn't intend to be different. Being childish is the sweetest and most harmless form of inferiority and those who infantilize children are welcoming them affectively in an inferior status, certain to have been given the duty to preserve them in that state. However, does anyone doubt the affection of overprotective adults? Affection exists unrealized, because it doesn't embrace the different. Derogatory affection preserves the different as different, only coming closer to it in order to make it inferior. Those who infantilize children do not take them seriously.

49 – EMOTIONAL NEEDINESS IS A FICTION OF THE IMAGINATION

Who has never wanted to be able to jump out the window and take flight? And who has ever felt depressed for not being able to do it? No one gets depressed for not being able to fly, even though it might be a great desire. We don't assign a possibility of realization to this desire. However, if people close to us were able to jump out the window and fly, not being able to do so would be frustrating to us. We attribute a possibility of realization to the desire to be professionally successful because many people are successful. In the face of other people's success, we may feel frustrated. However, what we know of other people's achievements is only an idea, because we don't experience them. And the idea of other people's achievements becomes our own ideal of accomplishment. If the criterion of our fulfillment is someone else's achievement – which we idealize – we believe we are only fulfilled when others also believe we are. That is why our happiness needs so many "likes" in social networks. If we can convince others that we are happy, it will be easier for us to believe it as well.

From an early age, we believe in the importance of the romantic ideal to happiness. Freud sees this ideal as the product of an ideal relationship between a child and his mother that was once lived and lost. We seek the realization of the romantic ideal to experience again what was lost. However, by definition, the real is opposed to the ideal, thus ideals are never – and have never been – lived. To the idealized past is added an imaginary component that is absent when lived, and this imagined past becomes the ideal of an impossible future.

If we had never known relationships from personal experience or the experience of others, would we ever adopt a romantic ideal? Would we ever suffer for being alone? Would we ever have the need of a loving partner? We adopt a romantic ideal because we see couples in relationships and imagine that they are happy because of it. And this imaginary happiness is sold to us by the TV and the movie theatre. The idea that we have of other people's happiness becomes our own ideal of accomplishment. We adopt this ideal as if there were no other way to happiness, and frustrate ourselves when we don't achieve it. "After all," we think, "how do people who date, get married and are therefore happy see us when we're alone? They certainly see us as unhappy". If they see us that way, we see ourselves the same way. The way we look at ourselves is the way we believe others look at us.

Many people can't find happiness in life as a couple, and still they insist, relationship after relationship, for believing there can only be happiness inside the ideal molds. They continue believing because, for them, there is no choice. They suffer in neediness for the lack of a relationship that they never experienced, and not only they imagine to have someday lived that relationship in a distant childhood, they also imagine this relationship is now being experienced by others. If only they knew their neediness is a fiction of their imagination…

50 – WHO IS RESPONSIBLE FOR OUR SUFFERING?

Are we free individuals or are we a product of the environment? This is an endless debate in Philosophy and Psychology. It is an endless discussion because these are two inconsistent alternatives, and scholars insist on choosing one. Although true, they are both one-sided alternatives. Freedom and determinism are not opposite ends. It is our task to understand their unity. If we didn't experience freedom, we wouldn't understand what it means to be tied to the circumstances; and if we didn't experience the imprisonment to circumstances, we wouldn't understand what freedom is. We only distinguish one opposite by distinguishing the other, as well as we only distinguish the heat from the cold because we know both. In the unfolding of destiny, we experience freedom and the determinant force of the circumstances. We cannot deny either one.

Ambiguity doesn't lie only in the relationship between subject and world. The relationship with the world is ambiguous because our subjective states are ambiguous. Desire, for instance, is experienced as a subjective state. The desire is ours; we desire. Because of the desire, we create wings and overcome that which oppresses us. However, the desire is experienced as an alien force in us and it dominates us against our will. It isn't awaken by our own will and we can't choose to make it stop. Thus, the act of desire is a manifestation of freedom and free will as much as it is a manifestation of imprisonment to circumstances that we cannot control. However, one cannot split desire into half freedom and half imprisonment; it is free and imprisoned as a whole. In the act of desiring, we are free within ourselves and, at the same time, prisoners as a whole. In our relationship with the world, we are also at the same time free of it and its prisoners. If we had been born in different conditions and lived in different circumstances, our lives would be different. But we were free and we are free in the choice of answers to what was offered to us, and life would also have been different if we had taken advantage of the possibilities of having acted differently. The anguish and repentance are proof that there were alternatives to our choice.

In short, suffering is our responsibility and the world's responsibility. The most common mistake in addressing this issue is to use the finding of liability of one side as an argument to invalidate the liability of the other. And the difficulty to condition the error is to understand how the responsibility of the two sides can overlap without having one defeating the other. However, it is even harder to avoid the indulgence and ruthlessness that mutually accompany the argument for the world's responsibility or the subject's responsibility. We cannot take away from a normal adult the responsibility for his actions, no matter how hard his life has

96

been. And we cannot disdain someone's suffering or treat him with insensitivity because we believe he is responsible for his own pain. Ultimately, we are all responsible for our suffering. And this doesn't make our suffering any smaller or less worthy of empathy. To point the finger and accuse someone of being responsible for his own suffering, as if this erased his deserving of compassion, is hypocrisy. Those who act as such draw a line between justified and unjustified suffering, placing others in the field of unjustified suffering while categorizing their own suffering as justified. For we only judge the suffering of others as unjustified if we believe that ours is justifiable. The indulgence that takes away from the person the responsibility for what he does is also hypocritical. Those doing it implicitly state that they could come to commit justified crimes themselves, if the external circumstances forced them to do so. Freedom is a paradox. That is why both behavioral psychologies and idealistic philosophies find it so difficult to understand it.

51 – THE TRUTH ABOUT OURSELVES IS IN THE RELATION BETWEEN OPPOSITES

In identifying with others, the Self can form its identity. The identity of the Self is its identity with others. However, the identity with others doesn't prevent others from being identified as different from the Self. On the contrary, insofar as the identity with others makes the Self conscious of its identity with itself, it makes it possible for the Self to distinguish all that is different from itself; and the other is by definition different from the Self. Nevertheless, if the identity of the Self is its identity with others, the others identified as different from the Self represent the difference of the Self in its identity with itself. The Self that is conscious of its identity with itself is different from itself. And if the Self is always aware of its identity with itself, then its difference with itself can only be unconscious. Unconsciousness is the difference of the Self with itself; difference of which the Self is not conscious. However, the unconscious is not necessarily a part of the mind excluded from consciousness. On the contrary, the unconsciousness of the Self's difference from itself is experienced in the consciousness-of-the-other identified as different from the Self. Psychoanalysis expresses this fact quite simply and allegorically by stating that the unconscious is "projected" onto the other.

The unconscious is the other within us. The other identified as different and exterior from the Self is the essence of the Self, because the Self is formed through the identification with others. So what the Self hates in others is its difference with the other not realized as identity of the Self (or as what the Self loves in others); and that which the Self loves in others is the identity with the other not realized as the difference of the Self with itself (or as what the Self hates in people). In short, the unconscious represents the other side, the opposite of everything we are and feel; in Jung's words, the unconscious is our shadow, the "negative" of the Self. In the analysis of the unconscious, what is desired appears as feared, whatever is feared appears as desired, what is loved appears as hated, what is hated appears as loved, certainty is doubt and doubt is certainty.

Consequently, the opposite of everything that we are, that we think and feel also exists in us. This ambivalence is essential in us and, it seems, we cannot get rid of it. So, how can we be true to what we feel and think? Truth goes through the humility of admitting that there is no absolute love or hate, there are no convictions without questions or doubts without conviction. Those who believe in the purity of their own feelings and convictions fall into contradiction. For the maturity of love, for instance, depends on the acceptance of that which is opposed to love in us; as well as the maturity of beliefs depends on the conscience of doubt. Opposites to which we refuse to allow access into consciousness dominate our attitudes without us realizing it. Those who deny the impurities of love live an idealized love that lacks respect for the loved one, despite contrary statements. Whoever denies the doubts that shake his beliefs and the uncertainties that erode his convictions are isolated in their own ideas and are far from reality, although convinced that they know the truth.

52 – THE WORLD'S MOST SERIOUS DISEASE IS NORMALITY

Some seek a psychologist because they are bothered by what they think and feel. They only reveal the contents of these – usually harmless – thoughts and feelings once they feel comfortable. After that stage, we expect the classic question: "Is that normal?" or "Am I crazy for thinking or feeling this way?". These are people who feel oppressed by a normality pattern in which they don't fit. The pressure of normality, at first an outer pressure, is then internalized, and exercised by the person upon himself. However, the internalized pressure goes back outside: those who feel oppressed by normality also constrain those who deviate from it. The difficulty in accepting one's own deviations reflects the difficulty of accepting other people's deviations, and vice versa.

The paradox of personality makes it difficult to escape the pressure exerted by normality. The identity of the Self is formed in the identification with others. Thus, the identity of the Self is the other. A person's Self is the other of himself. In other words, the Self is different from itself. The other is both the identity and the difference of the Self from itself; it is that which we believe we should be but we are not – or believe we aren't. Consequently, we fear revealing to others what we think and feel. We consider our thoughts and feelings inadequate to the standard represented by the other, and strive to behave in front of them in the way we deem most appropriate. However, it is essential that the other also doesn't deviate from this pattern. Our identification is linked to the standard represented by the other, and the deviations between one thing and another may endanger the preservation of our identity. Therefore, those who exert the pressure of normality upon themselves will also do it upon others. Thus, the pressure of normality is exerted (1) by the other upon the Self; (2) by the Self upon itself; (3) by the Self upon the other; (4) by the other upon himself.

Normality is based (1) on the fear of revealing to others what we are and (2) on the subsequent expression of a pattern of inauthentic behavior. No one who behaves within normal standards fits in this pattern. In one of his most quoted passages, Freud says, "Viewed up close, nobody is normal." We don't need to get too close. For the wise, observing that we embarrass each other in order to meet the standards of normality is enough to conclude that no one does. Going back to psychotherapy patients, a few are aware that they strive to fit in a behavior pattern that is inauthentic to them. They are aware that this way of living doesn't make them happy, and still prefer it to the harmless deviation from a fictitious normality. How can one avoid anxiety in such conditions? We can't escape from anguish when the opportunity of an authentic life knocks at our door and we reject it. Depression or anxiety are inevitable. If all anxious, depressed, medication-dependent people were analyzed by competent psychologists, how many analyses would reveal a strenuous effort to live inauthentically? Not all strive consciously and voluntarily, but everyone experiences the anguish of unfulfilled life.

Normality is a collective disease; the only one in which we are victims, infective agent and transmitting agents at the same time. With it, we poison ourselves and others and block everyone's access to an authentic life. For this reason, normality is the most serious disease worldwide.

53 – VANITY IS THE PUREST ESSENCE OF THE SELF

The opposite of low self-esteem is not high self-esteem. The opposite of low self-esteem is pride or vanity. Pride and vanity are almost synonymous expressions. Both emphasize different perspectives of egocentrism. Whereas pride designates an opposition of the Self to all that it sees as loss of self-worth, vanity points to the satisfaction found in what is seen as a gain of that worth. What is curious in vanity is the criterion used by the Self in assessing self-worth gain: a vain person is only satisfied when he thinks his worth equals that of others, but for his worth to become equivalent to the worth of others, others must first recognize him as superior. Thus, those who are vain only feel equal to others when their worth is recognized by others as superior to their own.

To the vain, it isn't enough simply being identified with others. It isn't enough sharing the same tastes and interests, the same social life, the same name, the same nationality, the same human condition. It is also necessary to feel superior somehow; and for the vain to feel superior, others must recognize their superiority. The simple identification with others is not sufficient for them to establish identity. How could it be? Identity is equal, and the other is by definition different from one's Self. How could the identification with others make me identical to what is different? The identity with the other is an unattainable ideal. The Self is bound to fall short of its ideal. So its identity with others is never complete, which leaves a residue of incompleteness. The residue of incomplete identity is the residue of equality ever achieved with the other, and the Self that does not reach equality with the other remains inferior.

But if the Self can't identity with the other, it is inevitable to conclude that the other doesn't conform to the identity with the Self. The other that doesn't conform to the identity with the Self is inappropriate to it, and therefore inferior. In the identification of the Self with the other, the other is both below me and above me. Thus, the Self must feel above the inferior other so that it feels equal to the superior other. But without the recognition of the other, the Self doesn't establish the identity with him. The other must recognize the Self as superior to himself so that the Self feels identical to the other. And the satisfaction of superiority duly recognized by the other is what we call vanity.

Vanity is the purest satisfaction of the Self. Without vanity, there would be no Self. Vanity is a consequence of the Self's nature, which is formed through its identification with those different form it. Humanity is not divided in vain and not vain people. We are all vain, without exception. So, how can we understand humility? It makes no sense to think of humility outside its relationship with pride and vanity, as well as there is no point thinking about the cold out of its relationship with heat. Humility is not the absence of pride or vanity. Humility is the behavior that

101

aims to avoid the negative consequences of vain and proud behavior. In this sense, it is indistinguishable from a kind of prudence. It is wiser to be humble than to be vain and proud. Humble behavior is always thought out and premeditated; very different from the free acting that can be only provided by the absence of pride and vanity.

54 – SHY AND EXTROVERTS ARE NOT WHAT THEY SEEM TO BE

We are always judging by appearance. However, this may not be the most prudent way to proceed. Especially in regards to people and their behavior. In our social life, we live with shy and outgoing people. Shy people keep themselves at a distance and speak little. Extroverts talk all the time and are always surrounded by people. If we judge by appearances, we'll conclude that the shy don't like people and that the outgoing love the crowds. And most of us think that way. But what if I told you that the reality is the opposite? I'm not saying that extroverts hate people and that introverts love the social life. Extroverts clearly show ease in dealing with people. Consequently, social life is no mystery to them, and they enjoy it easily. Introverts lead poor social lives in most cases, and get from it as much joy. So it seems that social life is more pleasant for the outgoing than for the shy. However, what makes extroverts launch themselves body and soul into everyday life is not necessarily sympathy and affection for others, and what makes the shy retract is not necessarily the lack of interest in people.

Both the shy and the extrovert are needy. And need is something that can hurt if left alone, but it can also hurt if we try to do something about it. Thus, the difference between introverts and extroverts is their attitude toward their own need. The shy are so scared that the exposure in social life will frustrate them even further that they prefer the risks of isolation. On the other hand, extroverts have such fear of being even more frustrated with isolation that they prefer the risks of social exposure. You can explain this difference by the circumstances of life, in some cases. Education, for example, can contribute in the constitution of a shy or an outgoing personality. However, children show traces of shyness or extroversion from birth. And while an outgoing child can become a shy adult due to education, the opposite is more rare to observe. A child born shy usually keeps his shy personality as an adult. Thus, we cannot explain the difference between shyness and extroversion considering only someone's life history, even though it might have been extremely relevant.

The difference in attitude between shy and extrovert people lies in how each focuses on his own neediness. In the relationship between the Self and the other, the Self comes into contact with itself and with the other. It comes into contact with itself through the other and with the other through itself. But the Self will also need to learn to detach from others in order to get in touch with itself and let go of itself in order to get in touch with others. For the shy, others are so important that they fear becoming null in the contact with people. In order to preserve themselves, they run for isolation. For the extrovert, their ego is so important that they fear it will become null in the contact with itself. In order to preserve themselves, they run for the crowd. The fear aroused from the contact with others manifests itself in social phobia. The fear aroused from being in touch with oneself manifests in the anxiety that accompanies one's loneliness. A shy person desires to fully surrender to others, body and soul. But to do so, he would need to let go of himself. Without this detachment, his need is experienced as a fear of becoming null in the relation with others and so he prefers to remain attached to himself and give up on others. An extrovert would like to surrender to himself, body and soul. But to do so would require letting go of others. Without this detachment, his need is experienced as a fear of becoming null in the relationship with himself and so he prefers to resign himself and continues bound to others.

Both timid and the extroverts lead an inauthentic life. And this inauthenticity is potentiated by the fact that they believe in the appearances of shyness and extroversion. Shy people commonly believe to be antisocial and to not like people; extroverts are commonly convinced that they nourish deep sympathy for others. They don't understand that social life causes so much distress to the shy and loneliness causes so much anguish to extroverts because both refuse to look for the authenticity that can only be found, respectively, in the relationship with others and with oneself.

55 – OUR ACTIONS HAVE MEANING ONLY THROUGH FREE WILL

Some schools of thought in Psychology and Philosophy reject free will. They want to explain man as a product of the environment or set man as a system responding to environmental stimuli. I believe that this definition would reasonably apply to a newborn. A newborn is practically devoid of autonomy. All his autonomy comes down to crying when unhappy. Only then he is asserting himself as a willful being in the world. And still, his cries could be explained as a response to the environment that left him deprived of something. Insofar as the baby begins forming his own identity, the situation changes. He becomes more autonomous in transforming the environment. But, we can still explain their behavior for environmental contingencies. This explanation begins to reveal its poorness when he enters the preteen years, showing itself increasingly inadequate from that point on.

Shortly after birth, we are unaware of our individuality. The world is our extension. Individuality is formed with identity, and the consciousness of our identity is formed with the consciousness of our difference from the world. While unaware of our individuality, we don't care much for being satisfied by the world. After all, the world is our extension. However, whereas our identity awareness forms itself with the consciousness of our differences from the world, the relationship between subject and world – marked in childhood by passivity at peace with itself – shall then be marked by the typical tense relationship between things mutually different. The tension between subject and world threatens the subject's identity. To continue building his identity in a world that now differs from him, the subject must overcome the tension, which requires effort, willpower, patience and self-control; in other words, it requires the development and the exercise of his autonomy. Tensions with the world brings to the subject the need to face it. Omitting to this confrontation makes one experience it as anxiety. Anxiety appears as we remain in our early childhood passivity that only responds to the environment not taking the active position of the subject that acts to change it.

The anxiety we begin to experience in adolescence is proof that we're not controlled by the world. Better yet, it is proof that we can't let the world control us. The realization of identity requires effort, patience and resignation; it requires us to take on our autonomy. Researchers who reject free will argue that environmental contingencies can be pointed out even in actions of effort; that even then we're nothing but a responding system. Clearly, there is only tension between a subject and the world because the world never ceases to put pressure on the subject. Thus, effort can be understood as a response to the pressure from the world. But if effort is understood as such, the entire true sense of the relationship is lost; the whole sense of effort is lost and reduced to a baby's passive action.

You can explain a person as a product of the environment or as a product of himself. And the explanation that takes people as products of the environment doesn't always do justice to their merits or demerits; this explanation doesn't always allow us to understand the meaning of their actions, and therefore doesn't always allow us to help them in the best possible way. We are surrounded by researchers and academics (not to mention also politicians, admen and media men) who would like to master men's knowledge as well as the instruction manual of a machine is mastered. It is our duty to react contrary to this. If we let ourselves be controlled like machines, we lose control over anxiety.

Tiredness and lack of time are the most common excuses to abstain from something. Most of the time, lame excuses. However, it could be the case that not enough time was given to plan an event and we were notified on short notice, which could be solved with better organization. Tiredness is different. We suffer from a fatigue from which we don't recover because we do not understand what's wrong with the life we lead; a life that makes little sense, and that pushes us like a snowball that began to form long ago. We can't find the words to put things in place. We are paralyzed in the face of a force that pulls us down and seems to make our feet weigh a ton. We don't know what to do. Our only desire is to sit back and let time pass. And when we try to talk about what's going on, the only word that comes out of our mouths is tiredness.

There is tiredness that is solved with a little organization. However, this kind of tiredness leaves us with a smile; the fatigue that arouses from dedicating ourselves to tasks that fulfill us. Such tasks can also make us exhausted, but all it takes is some time off so that everything is resolved, and the pleasure of returning to our activities will be as rewarding as or even more rewarding than having taken a rest. Nevertheless, there is a different kind of tiredness: the kind we carry with ourselves even when taking some time off and that makes vacation seem like an escape attempt, rather than simply relaxing time.. It is the tiredness that doesn't give us rest and makes us desperate in the face of returning home. What makes this tiredness poisonous is the difficulty to find words that will bring sense to it. If we could talk about it, we would know what to do. Not put into words, it turns into anguish. Anguish is fatigue residue that remains after vacation. We don't understand how tiredness can still remain after so much fun and why we experience it as a pinch of desperation when we remember we're coming home.

Those who don't express their fatigue in words blame other people, the routine, their work, the way back home. They blame everyone and everything, finding the solution in the radical change of the world around them. It is true that we might have to end some relationships, find a different job or make other objective

106

changes in order to find authentic rest. However, that doesn't mean changing the world, but our relationships with it. We can't find the words to talk about tiredness because we don't realize that our relation with the world can be changed. If we're not aware of what needs to be changed, there are no words to explain the dissatisfaction with that which hasn't yet changed. As a result, we get this tiredness that doesn't give rest – since the relationships that produce this fatigue don't change – and about which we can't speak – since there is no awareness of what needs to be changed. Tiredness explains nothing; it needs to be explained.

57 – OUR TRAGIC PURSUIT OF INTIMACY

The ideal of establishing a perfect relationship is in our list of priorities. We seek for exchange, trust and intimacy, but we follow the script of a tragedy. Our search fails due to its own efforts. Indeed, if there were no distancing there would be no need for approximation effort. If the effort to approximate is real, distancing is also a reality. Consequently, there is only closeness when there's no more effort. One can imagine that the effort decreases as the proximity is built. However, the effort to get close does not produce approximation. The greater the distance, the more urgent the desire for intimacy, but distancing is a consequence of the fear to reveal ourselves to others. In oppression and in the loneliness of fear, we fantasize intimacy as deep and harmless, at the same time. Thus, if the effort to get closer exists only in the distance, and distancing only exists in the fear of exposure, the approximation effort will be a result of the fear that conditions the distance. The goal of the effort is to establish deep intimacy within harmless limits to the fear of exposure. Therefore, the approximation effort is doomed to failure because there's no intimacy in a place where the fear to get close prevails.

The desire for intimacy is the product of loneliness, which is a product of the fear to get close. The stronger the fear, the stronger the desire for intimacy, and the more fanciful the desired intimacy.

107

Imagination is free to create, and in its right to create, it designs unreal forms of intimacy. Unreal because they're dictated by fear. Fear distances us from reality, and all that is based on fear is marked by eccentricity. Besides being eccentric, intimacy based on fear is contradictory: we seek the intimacy we fear and, although imagination is free to imagine it devoid of conflict, in practice, conflict arouses.

When the approximating effort conflicts with the fear of establishing intimacy, there are two possible outcomes: (1) frustration will make us bitter and prone to blaming others; (2) we'll become obsessed with intimacy. Personally, I prefer bitterness. Bitter people accept, albeit superficially, the inability to carry out their fantasies. In turn, obsessive people can't admit to leave their fantasies aside. Their approximation attempts result in frustration and anxiety, and the more frustrated and anxious, the more obsessive their search becomes.

Intimacy is no exchange of secrets, confessions and mutual promises of eternal fidelity. Intimacy exists spontaneously when there's no fear. No effort is necessary in getting closer to infants or animals. And yet, no one exchanges secrets or confessions with them. Proximity with babies and animals is based on the absence of fear. We have no reservations around them. Nowadays, people feel more intimate with pets than with each other. Besides proving that intimacy only exists in the absence of fear, this also demonstrates our inability to get closer to each other.

58 – LEARNING TO SUFFER IS ESSENTIAL

I have been paying attention for a while now to what I call "the Christmas syndrome": the dull air and general sadness that prevails in the Christmas celebrations of some families. We're bombarded yearly by the romantic vision of Christmas where people have fun together, resolve long-term conflicts and live happily ever after, but the contrast between fantasy and reality saddens some. We take on the obligation to have the perfect Christmas as seen in movies and, if Christmas isn't perfect, it won't do. However, perhaps the Christmas syndrome is taking over us all year long. We increasingly believe that we must live happily all the time. Consequently, inevitable sorrows seem like a transgression. Suffering is not allowed. This is so serious that we can't tell how much suffering comes from facing a real and painful situation and how much suffering comes from the difficulty to peacefully accept it. People suffer because they can't handle being in pain.

Some people despair not so much because of the painful situation, but because it brings them suffering. When these people seek the psychologist, they expect immediate relief or at least a guaranteed happy ending. However, the psychologist can only help them face adversities in the best possible way. I've seen some become disappointed after hearing this. They usually don't return for the next session. But I've seen the joy in the smile of many. After all, it is rare to find someone who won't console us with fibs. Addressing the situation in the best way is learning how to suffer. Those who don't welcome the lack become dependent on the abundance, when it exists. Those unable to suffer through the lack suffer from the fear of losing what they have. Peace only happens when you live serenely in the absence and without attachments to abundance. We must learn to suffer, not because suffering has a positive side, but because learning to suffer is the way to mitigate suffering. The absence of suffering is what's positive and good, not suffering itself.

We can't eliminate suffering by taking drugs (whether they are legal, illegal or prescription drugs); suffering doesn't go away with daily doses of renewed hope; suffering isn't eliminated with nights out, shopping sprees or trips; one can't eliminate the pain of a great loss with a replacement part. The only way to eliminate suffering is with calm, patience and a down-to-earth attitude. Suffering is the reverberation of reality attacks to our pretensions, our desires, our naivety; it is reality invading the dreamlike slumber in which we live, and you can't fight reality with escapism. If it were possible to escape from reality, reality wouldn't make justice to its own name. One can only face reality by firmly keeping both feet in it, and that requires patience and humbleness to accept that we're not too good to suffer. When sadness is welcomed with serenity, we put a smirk and announce the start of a new day.

59 – WHEN SUFFERING BECOMES THE MEANING OF LIFE

The desire to live pushes us by the realization of our identity in a world that is different from us and, since the difference that separates us from the world cannot be suppressed, there is still frustration even in the greatest achievement. To become mature is to become able to assimilate frustration with serenity. But ingenuity and idealization of dreams hinder the acceptance of inevitable disappointments. To the naïve and idealized desire, even small disappointments take on great proportions. Great disappointments need major problems to justify themselves. In their absence, they are invented. We unnecessarily make life complicated; we feel bothered by everything and everyone, we change what needs not to be changed, we blame those who aren't guilty of anything just to justify the dimension created around the simplest disillusionment. Minimum setbacks acquire tragic extent. Everything becomes offensive and disrespectful, all seems absurd; everything should be different than it is.

The difficulty in peacefully assimilating disappointments may induce the belief that all we live are illusions. And the intuition that life is illusory can be unbearable. Those who believe they live in an illusionary world can yearn for discovery of something undoubtedly right. And how do we find certainties in an illusory life except for destroying its illusions? Only disillusionment can break through the veil of illusions and uncover reality. Thus, paradoxically, the difficulty in accepting disappointments can makes us stuck to what disappoint us.

It's like a woman who suffers in her marriage but can't leave her husband. She believes in the ideal of love, and has to suffer for it. Her suffering won't allow her to fulfill her ideal, and consequently won't let her forget that it is only a dream. There's also that woman dating a man who doesn't treat her with the consideration she desires. She's always complaining and dreaming of an attentive

110

boyfriend. One day, she breaks up with her cruel boyfriend and finds the long-expected loving man. For a while, they live a fairy tale, but as time passes, some things change. Something is wrong, and she doesn't know what it is. Suddenly, she starts feeling bothered by her boyfriend. Finally, the relationship can no longer resist. She leaves him and meets another man, much like the first, thus returning to the same suffering and the same complaints she wanted so bad to get rid of, but that make her life seem real.

When dreams are naïve and idealized, small disappointments are great threats. To preserve them, we need to keep them away from anything that could potentially make them come true, because their realization requires maturation and maturation requires the acceptance of small disappointments. The most effective way to distance a dream from becoming true is to make it hostage of hopelessness, because hopelessness is the only disappointment that preserves the ingenuity and the idealization of dreams. Thus, those not ready to suffer small disappointments become hostage to the great pain of hopelessness, and when hopelessness occupies the place of realization, it must be grand and idealized, like the dream it preserves unrealized. By taking the dimensions of great despair, small disappointments acquire the mythological sense of a Greek hero's deeds. Those who don't learn to suffer enjoy bragging about their own suffering and don't accept criticism from anyone, because only they "know the hard way through which they came". They create a mythology around themselves and transmit it orally and in writing. Looking around, it seems we live surrounded by modern versions of Hercules.

Those who have learned how to suffer, keeping both feet firmly on the hot ground without excuses, don't brag about their own pain. They can make their dreams come true and know how to get rid of suffering at the first opportunity, never returning to it. Suffering is only glorified by those who never allowed themselves close enough to truly know it and all that is known only from a distance will remain shrouded in mysterious mist.

It is a common feeling to know what is wrong, to know what to do to fix it, and still not knowing how to do it. Many psychotherapy patients expect the psychologist to tell them how to change what they want to change. Some have accurate explanations. They understand the consequences of their behavior, they understand how their own reaction to the consequences reinforces them and they know what to change so that this vicious circle is broken. Nevertheless, it all still seems mysterious. They identify the problem, but they're still attached to it. While understanding the causal relationship between their own behavior and what bothers them, they still believe they have reasons to behave that way. Understanding what has to be changed in our way of doing things is not enough if it still makes sense to us. If our reasons still seem justified, the most elaborate explanations remain useless. We will continue with the feeling of knowing what to do without knowing how to do it.

We can only change something that, for us, has lost its reason for being. Therefore, as long as we find reason in what needs to be changed, we will continue not knowing how to make the change. This sets a clear limit to what a psychologist can do. The patient needs to dispose of the reasons he still claims to have to act the way he wants to change. To do so, the reasons need to no longer make sense. However, the psychologist can't transmit this lack of meaning to the patient. The psychologist transmits words. If the meaning attributed to words is enough to make them intelligible, but not enough for the patient to abandon his reasons, the psychologist can't really take any direct action. Only the patient can remove the sense of his reasons. The psychologist can help allowing him to talk freely and find unrealized meaning in the words spoken. The psychologist can make notes to assist the construction of meaning that will result in the removal of resistant reasons, but the effectiveness of his aid depends on the patient. There is no recipe, no technique, scientific or otherwise, to ensure the result. The success of the process lies in building a sense attributed only by the patient, whose autonomy is so autonomous that is beyond his control.

The process of building meaning is mysterious. Hence, Freud named its final act "insight". When meaning becomes clear, it illuminates consciousness at once. The patient needs to be engaged in the process, but the insight is not an act of his will. It expresses an autonomy that is free enough to get out of hand. Thus there is no indefectible recipe in the absence of the meaning required to make a change. The patient needs to be allowed to talk, and he must use the understanding of the problem as an aid in the change effort, even though the fear of change might still preserve meaning to the reasons to be abandoned. The effort can produce the "insight", but it will never produce an answer as to how to make the change. Waiting for a formula on how to do it is like being on the edge of a cold pool trying to figure out how to jump. The effort can encourage us to jump and the leap may come as an "insight", but if we don't stop thinking about how to jump, we'll spend the rest of the day staring at the water.

61 – CONVENIENCE IS PERFECTION'S WORST ENEMY

One bird in the hand is worth two in the bush, the saying goes. On certain occasions, it is wiser to accept what we have rather than to dream about what we don't. But this principle isn't always applied wisely. According to Kant, the good understanding properly applies a particular rule to each particular case. This obviously includes the ability to recognize cases in which the rule just doesn't apply. However, we have the habit of distorting everything – including popular sayings – using them as an excuse not for the best course of action, but for the most convenient one.

Convenient is what gives minimal satisfaction with maximum security. In this sense, what's best gives us maximum satisfaction with minimal security. It is part of the human tragedy that the best possibilities hold the biggest threats. Something that can provide great satisfaction can also turn into terrible frustration. In indulging in a great passion, we face the possibility to find the meaning of life and to lose all meaning at once. We may find intense acclaim or great rejection in expressing what we truly think. The possibility of freedom or anguish lies in the questioning of traditional truths. But how many of us prefer to just carry on with a colorless, unflavored relationship, from which we never really experienced anything special, only because we have become accustomed, or because the two families have become friends, or because the fear of taking the risk of solitude to find something better is greater than the desire to find someone else? How many of us prefer to express ourselves only when we're sure we'll be accepted because we believe that politeness requires eternal agreement, because we don't want to embarrass anyone with controversial opinions, or because the fear of disapproval is greater than the desire for an authentic contact? How many of us simply accept traditional truths just because they seem the most beautiful, because we've been raised to believe in them, or because the fear of leaving safe grounds is greater than the desire to seek something more meaningful? In all these cases, we are observing the "one bird in the hand is worth two in the bush" principle, and we are doing it the wrong way.

The convenient is always useful. There is much use in the convenient romance, in convenient friendships, in convenient truths. Convenient choices keep us away from complications we willingly avoid, whenever possible. In a world governed by convenience, meaning is sought in the utility. And when all meaning is sought in the utility, the very utility of the meaning is lost. The best romance is not the convenient one, but one in which the other's presence means being together. The best friendship is not a convenient one, but a friendship in which the exchange of differing views results in an agreement with yourself. The best truth is not a convenient truth, but the truth that leaves us no choice but to search for completeness in the void once occupied by anguish. The best romance, best friends, the best reality are the ones that give meaning to life. There is nothing more useful than a life full of meaning. And the meaningful life is always here and now, within reach. It is not found in convenience or utility, for the convenient is only useful for reasons that lack meaning. And if we can have a meaningful life in our hands, why chase what's not?

I didn't live other times than these. I don't know how people lived in other times. But I know how they live today, and I can say that we are in the era of false contentment. We are afraid to look honestly into our lives; we are afraid to recognize we don't live well. We cling to what is good to fill the holes that distress us, isolating ourselves on a small island surrounded by an ocean of despair. In the impossibility to navigate, the attachment to the island is meaningless, even though it seems safe. We would only feel complete if we would learn to navigate. This is the most sensible conclusion we can take from isolation, and also the one we most rarely come to. We cling to the island as if it were more valuable than the entire unexplored ocean that surrounds it. And so we pretend to live, making us prisoners of an empty contentment to which we cling desperately.

Trapped on a small island, the threat of being swallowed by the murky waters that surround it is constant. Therefore, the prisoners of false contentment desperately cling to the hope that they will never be swallowed, desperately attached to the hope of being saved. However, the threat is still present even in the greatest hope. And when despair turns hope into hopelessness, hope is then broken, becomes depressed and loses its place. The prisoners of the false contentment know that it depends on few and fragile conditions: a romance, a job, good physical conditions, status. And when contentment is maintained by unstable conditions, one lives desperately attached to the elusive hope that everything will remain as it is.

There is no sense in hope. If there is hope in the future, there is hopelessness in the present, and only the present makes sense. Only by navigating the ocean of despair around us would we be able to realize now the meaning sought in hope. However, we cling to hope in order to escape facing this challenge. We attribute

115

meaning to hope by idealizing the false contentment. We make what's small into grand, what's false into true, not here and now but in the future. Hope is the idea of finding something true on the small island where now lies what's fake, the idea of the small becoming great even without confronting the vastness around us. Hope is magical thinking, it is fool's gold. If its foundation is false contentment, how could there be any truth in it? Attached to this false contentment we cling to the false future contentment, while the expected grandiosity remains untouched in our idea, never becoming real. It is a sad burden to depend on what's false to endure it.

63 – SUFFERING IS ALWAYS THE SAME TO ALL

There's nothing like being an expert on something. Having special training on a given subject transmits security. It's as if the specialization meant greater knowledge and competence. In Psychology, there are professionals who introduce themselves as experts in the various categories of psychiatric diagnoses. They are experts in borderline, bipolar disorder, obsessive compulsive disorder, etc. But that does it mean, for example, to be an expert in borderline disorder? In my opinion, it means the ability to accurately understand the suffering of someone who has the borderline disorder. And how can the expert truly understand it without experiencing it? If there is no similarity between the suffering studied by the psychologist and his personal suffering, nothing that he learned will make any sense. This is also the relation between his suffering and that of the depressed, obsessive, bipolar, etc. If the psychologist is able to understand the suffering of diagnosed patients, there are similarities between his suffering and theirs. The suffering of each of us is similar to all, no matter which life experiences separate us from others or which diagnoses differentiate us from them.

Suffering is always the same for everyone. There are many ways to talk about this universal suffering and it can have many names. Psychoanalysis calls it lack or castration; existentialist lines speak of the fear of death. I prefer to call it loneliness. Those who acquire a disability certainly suffer for the constraints they face and the difficulties of learning. But nothing would make a person suffer so much if it wasn't for the feeling of being far different from others, or the feeling of being excluded from the normal world. And what is this feeling but loneliness? Those who lose loved ones or fear losing them suffer from the emptiness left by the other's absence – loneliness. Those who fear death itself fear for the lack of everything and everyone that give meaning to their existence – loneliness. Jealousy is also a reaction to the threat of abandonment. Anger is a reaction to frustration. Therefore, all failure and disappointment are forms of loneliness. These are moments when we feel isolated in a world that refuses to look at us. My life experience differs from that of others. I have experienced and still experience painful situations that others have not yet experienced, and vice versa, but the essence of suffering is the same. Its different forms are variations of the same theme.

So why is it difficult to understand somebody else's pain? If the universal suffering is loneliness, and loneliness is the condition of being isolated from others, it isn't impossible to understand the suffering of others while we ourselves are suffering. How do we understand others if we are isolated from them? It is our own loneliness that prevents us from understanding other people's loneliness. It is our own loneliness that makes other people's loneliness seem strange and enigmatic to us. It is our own loneliness that makes human suffering a matter mastered by specialists only. A lack of familiarity with the suffering of others is not expressed only by psychiatric diagnoses. The very existence of the psychologist is proof of how miserably human is the world where the understanding of suffering is a professional skill. In an ideal world, everyone would be able to understand it. However, a world in which other people's loneliness would be understandable would be a world without loneliness; it would, therefore, be a world where there would be no more pain. Although "psi" professionals and diagnostics are a necessity, nothing justifies the abuse and the inability with which psychologists and psychiatrists make use of their work tools. Psychologists and psychiatrists, despite all their formal education, need to understand that one needs to overcome his own suffering to understand the pain of others, and that this overcoming only occurs in the open field of the world, not within the four walls of the university.

64 – RESPONSIBILITY AND GUILT ARE NOT THE SAME THING

There is no freedom without responsibility. Being free doesn't mean doing whatever you want, but making choices without restrictions. It is, above all, the ability to take responsibility for what you do and what you are. One must learn to be free. And how do we learn to be free in the midst of so many obstacles and hindrances? How do we learn to be free when social inequalities separates us from birth? How do we learn to be free in a world where so many are born slaves and prisoners? How do we learn to be free if we suffer the consequences of other people's actions? It is no easy task. In general, the learning of freedom occurs with shortcomings. When freedom is learned successfully, we learn we're responsible for what we are and what we do even though we live in a world that constrains us. When it is learned with deficiencies, instead of understanding responsibility, we craft the concept of guilt.

Freedom is not denied when we allocate in others the guilt for what we are and what we do. Guilt is only present when freedom – supposedly hindered – is still exercised. Guilt is attributed by freedom resented, freedom that couldn't be free. The resentful freedom doesn't take responsibility for its hindrance, and ceases to be free. It projects the responsibility onto the world that, carrying the weight of a responsibility that isn't its own, becomes guilty. People can also take on their shoulders the responsibility of others. There is guilt when one imputes to others his own responsibility or when one carries other people's responsibility. Guilt is the lack of measurement in the distribution of responsibility.

Guilt is never allocated unilaterally. Those who blame others also blame themselves and if one blames himself, he also blames others. Those who blame the world for what they are or do

118

implicitly assumes that he should be or act differently; thus assuming the blame for not being or not acting as he should. Whoever blames the world for what he is blames himself for not being good enough for the world. They allocate in the world the guilt of his own flaws, and therefore confess having failed with the world. In order for the world to be at fault, he must have had his own flaws. If he had not failed, it would make no sense to blame the world. It was he who failed the world. In turn, those who blame themselves for what the world is implicitly assume that the world should be or act differently, blaming the world for not being or not acting as it should. Those who bear the world's blame on their own shoulders blame the world for not being good enough for them who, now, bears the guilt of the world. The world has failed to adapt to them.

If the guilt I allocate in the world is the same that I carry in me, it belongs to no one. It doesn't exist. There is only the responsibility that each one of us must take – in the right amount – so there can be freedom without resentment.

65 – SUICIDE IS THE OTHER'S MURDER

Most people enjoy life, struggle to enjoy it or at least pretend to enjoy it. However, even for those convinced of its value, life is full of frustrations. Even in the great pleasures and in the achieving of great dreams there's also frustration. And it couldn't be different. When we seek the realization of our identity in a world different from us, the reality will always be different from our expectations. Still, the desire for full satisfaction remains vigorous. It is the desire to live fully without barriers and frustrations. And since life realizes and frustrates itself at the same time, the desire to live it fully will cling to it and, at the same time, strive to get life out of the way. It finds life is an obstacle to the full life it aims to accomplish. In this sense, the wish to die is a variation of the desire to live.

But the wish to die also contradicts the desire to live. Hence, those who are convinced they love life experience the wish to die

119

as a fear of dying. The more they cling to the conviction that they love life as to deny their wish to die, the more their frustrations become anxiety, and the idea of death begins to involve a panic that is too hard for them to elaborate. Frustrations are never absent, and the unconscious wish to die expresses itself in chronic anxiety and a fear of death that they can never get rid of. They say they love life, but never cease thinking about death. Therefore, when the wish to die is indeed experienced as such, the tables are turned. People with suicidal tendencies claim to love death, but never cease thinking about life; they never cease thinking of the fulfilled life they would like to live but are not able to. They love death because it presents itself to them as the only way of life; the only chance to escape a life in which the desire to live became unbearable. And just as the unconscious death wish manifests itself as anxiety for inveterate life lovers, for death worshipers the unconscious fact that the life they want to abandon is the same life they desperately want to live manifests itself as depression or melancholy.

If the wish to die is the distorted expression of the desire to live, the Self that wants to die actually wants to stay alive; better yet, it wants to eliminate the obstacles in the path to its realization. The identity of the Self seeks fulfillment in the world that differs from itself. The world is the identity of the Self. Since the world and I are identical, the elimination of the Self means the destruction of the world that prevents it from being fully me. Suicidals are prisoners of the fantasy that their death will be the end of the world. They wish for the end of the world even though they're aware that their suicide won't destroy it.

The world is represented by those around us. Thus, the fantasy of destroying the world by suicide means to assassinate the other who is blamed of our ills. The desire to murder the other expresses itself consciously in the intention to make him to feel remorse for the suicide. And in the deterred forms of this fantasy prevails the understanding that this evil can indeed occur, but temporarily; that all will find means to continue living and the only person definitely dead will be the one who committed suicide to kill others.

120

The wish to die is part of the desire to live. A fulfilled life is found in the harmony between the two paradoxical sides of life, something that is difficult for our unilateral consciousness.

66 – WHY IS IT SO HARD FOR US TO SAY "NO"?

"No" is one of the first words we learn. It expresses the establishment of boundaries between the Self that's in formation and the world. The child, so far passive, now begins to set limits for those who once did with him whatever they wanted. The word "no" is the birth of individuality. Every incipient individuality is still fragile. Being fragile and born into a world that is hostile to all individuality, it will surely suffer difficulties. Other people's individuality bothers us, for our Self is formed through the identification with the other. In this scenario, the other's individuality means the negation of our own identity, the lack of individuality. The lacking individuality makes no distinction between itself and the individuality of others. It wishes to submit it to its own will so that the other may think, feel and act in order to satisfy the nuances of his identification with it. The Self must mature to overcome the frustrations of its relationship with others' individualities. However, adults are still needy and can't distinguish between their individuality and that of others. Thus, when a child is born, he becomes easy prey for his parents' malformed individuality.

The needy adult can become authoritarian and possessive. Authoritarian people, incapable of distinguishing their own individuality from that of others, believe that children must obey them without questioning. Questioning is an expression of an individuality that wasn't consented to. Possessive people, also unable to distinguish their own individuality from other people's, believe that the child should always be willing to both receive all the love they might want to give and to give them all the love they demand. Refusal is an act of rejection. Thus, the child's "no" bothers both the father who sees in critical childish ways an act of outrage and disobedience and the old aunt who demands kisses

121

and feels rejected by the child's embarrassed resistance. The adult's discomfort is a threat to the child, because if the adult has a needy, malformed individuality, the child's individuality is still fragile and in training process. Hence, if even adults feel threatened by questioning or rejection, the child is much more likely to feel threatened by other people's discomfort, since, unlike adults, the child's physical existence depends on his relationship with others.

The hostile reaction to the child's "no" leads him to a dead end. The "no" sets the limits needed so that his individuality can constitute itself, but also puts him in danger. In facing it, the child has two alternatives: to feel intimidated or to rebel. However, intimidation and defiance are two sides of the same coin. Bullied children live indignant and rebellious children feel intimidated and threatened. The indignation and intimidation are the origins of individualism, for the indignant and the intimidated see others as contenders. Therefore, in a world hostile to individuality, individualism arises freely. The obsession to imprison the other is such that we learn to live based on the every man for himself approach.

67 – ETERNAL LIFE WOULD SOLVE NOTHING

Our identity lacks reality, thus it seeks realization. It seeks fulfillment in the world; a world that differs from it. To realize means making something real. Thus, our identity seeks to become real in a world that is different from it. The identity that seeks fulfillment in the world aims to become similar to it. And the effort to become identical to the world that differs from itself keeps it unfulfilled. Our identity is unrealized; it lacks reality. This lack is anguish. Anguish is the identity's lack of reality. And the identity that lacks reality leads a life that seems rarefied. Anguish is the feeling of thin air, the feeling that life lacks safety and foundation; finally, it lacks reality. But where is life's lack of foundation, of security, or of reality? As soon as we discover the existence of death, the answer is undeniable: life has no reality because we are mortal. It is unfounded because we can die at any moment, and if we can die at any moment, we can't feel safe in life. Since we don't feel safe, we live in anguish.

The identity that lacks reality suffers from loneliness. The life that lacks reality suffers from the fear of death. Our lack of reality has an obvious consequence: if we lack reality, we will seek the reality we lack outside of us. In solitude, we seek reality in a reality that will never be ours, because other people's reality will always be theirs. Similarly, if life lacks reality, seeking the reality of an after-life doesn't solve the problem. Hoping there will be life after death and that this life is eternal doesn't solve the anguish, for anguish is the lack of reality that erodes one's identity. Thus, death is not a cause of anguish, and eternal after-life wouldn't make it stop. We project onto death the blame for anguish because this is the most simplistic way to understand the issue. If life is anguished, then death holds the blame because it destroys life. However, anguish exists in life, not in death. It exists not because of life's future ending, but because of the lack of fulfillment of today's life. If we were immortal, our anguish would be the same, for the lack of accomplishment today would be the same. In that case, we would have to blame something else, not death. What would we choose to project the blame onto? We would certainly find something to blame. We do this all the time! In addition to blaming death, we always invent other problems and point out other culprits for these ills that never abandon us.

If immortality were enough to resolve anguish, it would also resolve loneliness, because loneliness is just another name for anguish. However, it is easy to imagine that there would still be loneliness in immortal life. Thus, if there is life after death and if it is eternal, our problems will also extend for eternity unless we resolve them now. If the cause of anguish is the lack of fulfillment in the present, putting hope in eternal extension of the after-life will not solve it. Life needs to become real now. Realization must happen now. Similarly, if life definitely ends with death, it won't be a problem. We don't suffer because life might come to an end; we suffer because it is so hard to achieve fulfillment. Life realized in the present doesn't care for the future; therefore, it doesn't face the possibility of dying as a problem. Finiteness is only problematic for unfulfilled life. Life is the problem, not death. Hence, Psychology must engage exclusively in life. Death will never be a problem for those who are truly alive.

68 – PESSIMISTS AND OPTIMISTS ARE MORE ALIKE THAN THEY SEEM

Fulfillment is always one step ahead of us. We search for it and expect it will come at some point. For one to foster expectation, one must believe the future holds the possibility of realization. If we don't see this possibility, we need to mature our patience and resignation. We often find ourselves in unpleasant situations that can't be resolved in the near future. In such cases, patience is the only thing that will prevent us from depression. But sometimes, even though there are realistic chances of a future of positive possibilities, we are tempted to say they don't exist and believe in negativity, because positive possibilities are not certain. What might work can also go wrong. And uncertainty is distressing. We value certainty over everything, and that includes the certainty of our everyday anguish; we're already used to it. However, expectation forces us to live with the possibility of frustration and the anguish that comes with that uncertainty hurts more than usual.

In life's capital moments, we are faced with a challenge: to abandon the usual anguish and soak in the anguish of uncertainty! Diving into the distress of uncertainty usually means physically and emotionally investing in projects whose success can have a huge positive significance for us, and whose failure may have a negative impact of the same proportion. Risks are always great. In the face of them, the temptation to opt for the usual angst is also great. However, in our eyes, rejecting the anguish of uncertainty and opting for the usual trouble demands a justification and, to justify our choice, we need to deny that future possibilities are real. Those who deny the existence of positive possibilities and profess their belief in the negative are called pessimist, and those who give body and soul to the belief of positive possibilities are called optimist.

Pessimists deny the existence of positive possibilities because they see the anguish of future uncertainty as unbearable. The mistake lies in thinking that optimists are different. Just as pessimists deny the existence of positive possibilities, optimists deny the negative; and they deny them because future uncertainty distresses them the same way. The optimist's motto is "positive thinking, always". Keeping in mind the idea that everything will work out is not allowing the possibility of something going wrong to reach consciousness. Both pessimists and optimists flee the challenge set by life in the capital moments; they both opt for the usual anguish and reject the anguish of uncertainty.

The pessimist turns negative possibilities into certainties: if there are no positive possibilities, then the negative ones are certain. The optimist turns positive possibilities in certainties: if there are no negative possibilities, then the positive ones are certain. In short, both pessimists and optimists deny the existence of possibilities; both affirm their belief in the certainty of the future to come. Realists, in turn, accept uncertainty. Contrary to pessimists and optimists, realists don't see uncertainty as a reason for unbearable anguish. Therefore, they don't turn uncertainty into certainties, whether positive or negative. Realists are people who, while accepting the future as uncertain, do everything in their power so that it can be positive, and are ready to receive it otherwise.

69 – WHY ARE WE SO SCARED OF ENVY?

Individuality develops as we build identity with each other. This is the most beautiful definition to human nature! We become individuals through communion with each other. Hence, the essence of man is a loving essence. However, it has its dark side. The differences between others and ourselves can make the affection train derail. Others' individualities are obstacles to our identity with them, and a threat to our own individuality. When other peoples' individualities threaten our own, the emotions we experience diverge from the love that characterizes communion with one another. Moreover, if the differences in the individuality

125

of others put them, in our view, in advantage or in a superior position to ours, envy might be the result. The other becomes target of our envy when he achieves or comes close to achieving ideals that we'd like to have achieved, because we then feel defeated in a competition we silently started. To mitigate the feeling of inferiority, the other must lose whatever he has gained. The other needs to go back and be beside us again – or better yet, well behind us – in the race of ideals. To envy is to wish for this scenario.

Among human emotions, few are as unconfessed like envy. It is also among the most hated. Envy is still quite feared. Hatred itself isn't so feared. The fear of envy is large enough to enter the sphere of mysticism. Some believe in the power of other people's envy magically causing them harm. However, there is an explanation for that. Of all negative emotions, envy is the least rational because it doesn't crave any benefit to the envious. Envious people want the person they envy to lose something without resulting necessarily in benefit for them. Therefore, rationally, envy seems unjustified. We are able to give many reasons why we hate. Hate can be justified in the harm the other caused us. Thus, hate turns against evil, wishing for the good of those who hate. We also attribute many reasons for the feeling of hurt. Hurt is the defense against the harm caused by the other. Its function is to prevent this harm from reoccurring. Jealousy can also have many reasons. Even though the reasons for jealousy might be imaginary or based on unfounded suspicions, they justify jealousy. Even though they might be hypocritical, all these justifications are plausible within our rationality. But what about envy? What justification is there to envy? When envy has as its target, for example, a direct opponent within a company, it can be called ambition or competitive spirit, and find justification, but how about when we target people whose success doesn't interfere in any practical aspect of our lives?

It's not easy to rationally justify envy. Among our negative emotions, it seems the most irrational. In its irrational condition, it is also the most feared. And fearing the irrational is also irrational. This explains the mysticism that involves the fear of envy. Its

126

apparent irrationality shows that our everyday rationality can't resolve subjectivity.

Children always have something to say; they always say what they feel, and their emotions run high with everything they experience. They are not afraid to say what bothers them; they're not afraid to say what they like and dislike. They don't have introspection capacity, they can't speak of themselves; they speak of the world that surrounds them, the things they see and hear, things that happen to them and to the ones nearby, but they speak only of what's important to them. Children don't make small talk. However trivial their interests may seem to us, they're important to them. They give signs of growing when they begin to choose what to say and start keeping their feelings away from the words, when they start to smile unwillingly and to talk about something uninteresting just to keep the conversation and preserve at a distance what really matters. They become adults when what's important is pushed aside and they no longer know how to talk about what they feel, or when they no longer know what they feel. Ultimately, they become adults when they learn to say "everything is fine" even when don't feel good, but are not quite sure what's wrong.

Children don't need to learn how to say what they feel. They can express themselves even before they learn to speak. They cry, laugh and smile according to what they feel. Their development to adulthood, from this perspective, is an unlearning process. Children must unlearn to say what they feel in order to adapt. They gradually learn that expressing their feelings has negative consequences. They find out their own emotions – positive or negative – are unsuitable for most situations. They learn that adults expect them a friendly and formal manifestation of a neutral and cheerful well-being, and so they learn to smile and say "fine" whenever they're asked how they are; they learn to be "fine" no

127

longer knowing what it means to be fine. They can learn to say they're well and to believe they are well, being unaware they aren't. They can also learn to say they are fine and have full awareness of not being fine, but not knowing how to express it. In the latter case, they learn to smile and say they're okay, even though they are silently crying for help. And they might not know how to cry for help, or maybe they know how to ask for help but don't know what to do when help is offered.

It is possible that we know we're not well and we ask for help without knowing what is wrong. Our situation might even worsen if help comes wrong. Those solicitous to help generally smother us with advices and exhortations that don't help us at all. We need to relearn how to say what we feel, restoring contact between words and feelings. We acquire this condition through constantly ignoring what we had to say because of what others told us to do, and that is why advices worsen even more the existing hurt. A great way of helping is often just to let us speak; better yet, it is to allow us to relearn to speak; which may not be easy. It's difficult to relearn how to talk about something that hasn't been perceived for a long time, it's hard to relearn how to talk about things that really matter when we talk only of trivial everyday occurrences: traffic, weather and work issues. Mostly, it is hard to learn to speak about ourselves when we only speak of others and when not even the children we once were could talk of those things. It is difficult to give importance to what we do when we only care about what others do. Finally, it is very hard to learn to be fine when "I'm fine" has become a meaningless expression.

71 – THE STRANGER LIVES IN US

When babies who used to always smile and allowed anyone to carry them around begin to cry in the presence of strangers, we say they began to reject those with whom they aren't familiar. Before this stage, no one seemed like a stranger, and no one's face was threatening. They smiled spontaneously even to animals and toys. The friendly naturalness with which they reacted to everything and everyone is lost when the familiar becomes safe and what isn't familiar becomes threatening. At first glance, there is no rationale in fearing the unfamiliar. Rationally, the fear is justified only because of past misfortunes. Therefore, we should only fear what has already become familiar. There is no point in fearing the unknown. There is consistency in this way of thinking, and despite the fear of the unknown disagrees with it in theory, a deeper analysis undoes this mistake.

A baby who starts to reject the unknown and becomes an adult who's used to fear the unknown will probably live without understanding that the target of his rejection is not unfamiliar things and people. Strangers are not frightening to the baby. The baby feels scared by the loneliness experienced in the absence of those he loves, and because the presence of strangers means the absence of those he loves, he feels alone in the presence of strangers. In the presence of strangers, the contact with oneself is unpleasant. The baby reacts negatively to strangers, but the cause of displeasure is the contact with himself, the loneliness. And he doesn't get used to this loneliness, even though it has already become familiar. This unlivable loneliness is the stranger who dwells inside. And since the contact with the stranger inside is conditioned by the presence of strangers or unfamiliar situations, those people and situations will be wrongly identified as the threat that exists only inside himself.

We fear confessing to others what is happening inside us. We fear they will reprove what we have to say; we fear they will think we're not normal. This fear is realistic. For the possibility of others rejecting us if we confess our intimacy is real, as is real the possibility of us rejecting others in the same situation. We are not used to getting in touch with other people's privacy because we're not used to having others getting in touch with our own. We feel threatened in the presence of what is abnormal in others for not knowing what is abnormal in us. And even though we know our abnormality, we don't get used to it. We do not accept it, we don't understand it. Therefore, we condemn it when we see it reflected in others. Nothing that is human should cause us rejection or estrangement. All forms of acting and thinking, including all forms

129

of sexuality, violence or cruelty are understandable if we don't fear seeing the other as an equal. For the strange other exists in us, even if we disagree with what they think or do. If the baby could once smile at all faces, even though different from his own – and so different among themselves – perhaps the potential to doing the same still exists within us.

72 – THE CRUELTY OF LOVE

Proximity is necessary to contact, and love is present in one of its forms wherever there is contact. However, where there is proximity there is also confusion and myopia, for perfect vision and a clear understanding rely on a certain detachment. In the absence of the clear understanding of what we feel, we open doors to cruelty. Thus, love can always fall into contradiction: the closer the contact, the more likely we are to get confused and treat our loved one with cruelty, cruelty practiced in the name of love.

Love confuses us because it is filled with fear. In love, we ideally realize the identity with the other. However, the idealized identity doesn't override reality: the other will always be the other, the other will never be me, and the identity with the other doesn't overcome the differences between him and me. If the other will never be me, he can at least be mine and, since having the other as mine is a prerequisite for the realization of identity with him, love soaks in attachment. In this attachment-soaked love, the threat of loss is unbearable. To mitigate it, it is necessary that the Self preserve the other as mine and, therefore, we must deny him the condition of being similar to itself. For the other similar to the Self is also an individual, and every individual is free. However, by taking it as mine, my Self denies the other his freedom and reduces him to a thing. Love objectifies the other. In the selfish satisfaction that takes the other as an object, love becomes cruel.

The love of the Self for the other it owns is characterized by possessiveness. The possessive Self imposes on the other the obligation to obey it. Obedience is rewarded and disobedience is punished. Disobedience justifies punishment, and the obedience's duty is based on the right of possession, a prerogative of love. The Self that loves its own other feels entitled to possess him, for the other grounds the identity of the Self, and the foundation's role is to sustain that which stands on it. Obedience is a condition for the Self to sustain itself on the other. In disobedience, the Self becomes insecure, and a foundation cannot cause insecurity to that which it sustains. Moreover, sustaining that which stands upon itself is not only the foundation's duty, but its only function. Foundations exist only to sustain. Without this function, its existence is meaningless. So in addition to obedience being a right of the Self, it is also necessary for the other. It's for the good of the other that the Self imposes obedience. It's for his own good that the Self forbids him to relate with those whom the Self dislikes. It's for the good of the other that the Self requires him to abandon all dreams for the achievement of the Self's own dreams. It's for the good of the other that the Self forbids him to distance himself. It's for the good of the other that the Self forbids him to stop loving the Self. And it is also for the good of the other that the Self reacts with jealousy, anger, destructive criticism and even physical violence every time he disobeys or threatens to disobey.

Nothing contradicts love better than love itself. Love is the need to consummate our identity with the different, and the impossibility of this actually happening, between two bodies, awakens the desire to, at least, possess our loved one for ourselves. But the possession of the other is illusory. Insecurity that is always tormenting those who love shows that ownership was never accomplished. The other was never mine; the other was and will always be his own. Walking toward true love begins with tears of detachment, but they immediately give way to the joy of finally finding peace in the freedom of the other.

73 – WE ONLY WISH TO BE VALUED FOR THAT WHICH WE ARE NOT

Everyone wants to be valued for what they are. But when people say they want to be valued, I can't really tell if they wish to have their personal value recognized or if they expect to be cherished beyond what they deserve to be. I'm pretty sure most people would answer they want to have their value recognized, but I suspect that, deep down, most wish to receive at least a higher value than that which is given to ordinary people. However, even if we admit each person's value is infinite, still there would not be someone worthy of a value greater than that of others. All infinities are equal; there is no infinity better or greater than another. But those who call for appreciation confesses believing they stand out from the crowd for who they are. What does that mean? Women want to find men who value them not for their appearances, but for their personality. Men want to find women who value them not for their social status, but for who they are. Those who feel passed over and gagged by society want to find some way to express themselves in order to be valued for who they are. It seems we all dream of finding that wise and sensitive person who, in a glance, is able to perceive in us all the beauty the world has always rejected; the beauty that was prevented from coming to light and that no one had yet noticed... not even ourselves. Yes. Apparently, we expect others to see in us a beauty that we don't. And why do we not see it? Because deep down we know that we would like others to see in us something that doesn't exist.

When we don't see in us the beauty we would like others to see, we imagine it and idealize it. In other words, we invent it, expecting someone will believe it. For we will always be, in our low self-esteem, dissatisfied with how others see us, no matter how beautiful or good others think we are. Such is the case of women who are always on diets, treatments and exercises to keep fit. They want to be desired and would like men to see in them ideal bodies that only exist in their imagination. In turn, a self-confident woman, who believes her own beauty and never struggled to attract attention, dreams of the man who will see in her an ideal person that, as well as the ideal body, also exists only in her imagination. The same goes for men and their relationship with social statuses and for anyone who's not satisfied with the look they get back from people. But low self-esteem makes us blind.

132

The woman who hopes to achieve the ideal body doesn't even realize she is already desired by the body she has, and the woman who expects to be loved for who she is doesn't realize she is already loved for the person living in her own body. However, in addition to making us blind, low self-esteem also makes us dissatisfied. Thus, once her own beauty starts drawing attention, the woman who fought for the ideal body will want to be loved for who she is. And having found a boyfriend who's romantic enough to believe he sees in her the ideal person she invented, the woman who wants to be loved for who she is will miss the time when she was loved for her beauty.

No matter how good our soul is or how sexy our body is. We will always be dissatisfied with the value we receive and we will always hope for an appreciation that goes beyond what we ourselves believe we deserve. We expect to be valued for who we are without realizing that 'who we are' means who we are not, and we want to be who we're not because our low self-esteem keeps us unhappy with anything we are. If we honestly loved ourselves, we wouldn't be billions of people dissatisfied for not receiving the special value we believe to be entitled to.

74 – WHEN STRESS BECOMES FOOD TO THE SOUL

Stress is not the name for simple everyday concerns, but for an apprehension that no longer finds rest, that warning sign that never turns off and has already become a habit. In our day-to-day, we fear everything. Death threatens us at every corner. Life is not safe; violence is everywhere. No one is safe. Those who have a job fear losing it, and those who don't fear they won't find one. Loneliness is also a threat both to those who are alone and for those who are not – or believe not to be. The cellphone ringing causes anxiety, the cellphone not ringing causes anguish. Receiving that awaited message brings a temporary relief for the uncertainty that never goes away. Noise is a constant companion. Even at night, there is always a car rushing on the street. Its rush is also ours. Why hurry? Outside, there is always someone speaking loudly, laughing, screaming. Inside, the noisy neighbor who walks heavy from one side to the other, drags furniture and drops everything on the ground. When will he stop? Maybe the right question is "will he ever stop?" The nearest neighbors are strangers, enemies who never speak. The streets are crowded with people who walk by each other without making eye contact; and the closer they walk by one another, the greater our desire that they will be further and further away. Today my hair looks good. What a glorious day! Tomorrow it won't stay. There's nothing good in this life! We visit the whole world and people from all around on social networks. And the fugacious laughter of a forced joke lives side by side with the anguish of finding everyone happier than I am. My online friends publish so many pictures laughing! Happiness is an obligation we never obey and always cheat sneakily. And the cheating never gets tiring.

I take the cellphone to bed with me, as well as the anxiety when it rings and the anguish when it doesn't. The joy of a received message goes away; the doubt that it might not mean what I'd like it to, stays. Noise gives a truce, but silence stuns my thoughts. And the neighbor, oh, the neighbor never stops. The streets are still crowded, yet we still don't feel close to one another. Proximity is feared, and distance too. Today my hair is good, but I'm worried about it tomorrow. No matter how much I believe that my life is good, life will always look better in my friend's pictures. And the fear of revealing our unhappiness to others is more important than fighting for happiness.

Greater than the fear of not having the cellphone ring is the fear of living without a cellphone. Greater than the nuisance of noise is the fear of living in silence. Greater than the discomfort of proximity and the isolation of keeping a distance is the fear to open up to the world. Greater than the constant worry about my hair is the fear of living in a world without aesthetic values. Greater than the anguish for my friend's happiness is the fear of discovering that their happiness is as false as mine. Greater than the fear of revealing my unhappiness to others or leaving in search of happiness is the fear of recognizing that in order to be happy, one would have to give up all these fears. And there is no greater

134

fear than the fear of abandoning all those fears. Not even death is more appalling. Not even hell could be worse than this so-called happiness. It isn't apprehension that never leaves us; we are the ones who fear abandoning it.

When stress becomes food to the soul, nothing stresses us out more than the opportunity to leave the stress; nothing is more uneasy than the fear of losing what makes us apprehensive. When the disease becomes an addiction, happiness seems a nightmare. This addiction is the essence of our lives, matter and form of our daily lives. We will fight to the end to preserve it and we will treat as enemies those who try to get us rid of it. Free of this addiction, we would only have to breathe. Free, all that'd be left would be life, and life is always next to nothing for someone who's gotten used to so little.

75 – CAN TRUE FRIENDSHIP EXIST?

The theme of friendship involves as many controversies as love. However, in our romantic society it is a little left aside. Our culture has always dedicated itself to the love theme. Works have been produced on love from ancient Greece, providing us with vast material for research and reflection. The same does not happen with friendship. I must speak of friendship only in the ways I have observed it personally. Therefore, I don't know what friendship meant fifty or a hundred years ago, but I can distinguish some features in friendships nowadays. First, it seems that some of us want to make our friends people to accompany us in our activities. This makes a friendship easily forgotten as soon as a more interesting company appears. The more interesting company may be another friend or romantic partner. Some of us commonly distance themselves from friends when we start dating, for example, and the distancing of some is repaid with the resentment of others. Second, it seems that we want as friends people with the same ideas and tastes we have. This makes many friendships end because of moral and ideological differences. Friends linked primarily by intellectual affinity interpret changes of opinion as treason. Third, it seems that we look for people who are loyal to us, not only in the good but also in the bad moments of life. And some of us resent when our friends act differently from we expected.

In short, the ideal friend is the embodiment of the trio "company + affinity + loyalty". Thus, it is easy to understand the difficulty of the theme "true friendship". Those who are most dramatic say that a true friend is the greatest gift one can achieve in life, but our friends will certainly leave us alone at times, they'll think and feel differently from us and act differently from what we expected. And if our friendship criteria is "company + affinity + loyalty", we will have to agree that keeping a true friend for life will be more difficult than finding an everlasting love. Friendship needs to have a different base. Because defining friendship by the trio "company + affinity + loyalty" is defining it by the usefulness of the other: a friend is one that serves as a companion, one that allows us to delight in our own ideas and that helps us when we need. A petty definition of friendship, that is! It is a mean and selfish definition, because it defines friendship by what a friend should represent to us when, instead, we should define it by what we feel for him.

Friendship shouldn't be defined by what the other represents to us, but for the affection we have for him. Consequently, we shouldn't count how many friends we have, but how many people we are friends of. Happy is not a person who has a true friend, but a person who's a true friend to someone, and being a true friend to someone is truly liking that person. Maybe that's why today's friendships are so fragile. People do not like each other. For how can we truly like someone when we expect the companion that never fails us, perfect affinity, and endless loyalty? Those who expect that much from others live frustrated and upset, and no affection springs and blooms in the aridity of frustration and annoyance.

Being around a disabled person may cause anxiety for those who are not used to it. Anxiety, in this case, has its cause in the same discomfort experienced by being around those who live in poverty or are depressed, for example. We must believe that happiness is a right and a natural consequence of life, and that any material or existential misery is the effect of personal choice or social conditions. In the case of the poor and melancholic, it's easy to find an explanation that puts the blame on some transgression of the sufferer or the society, but in the case of a disabled person, it's different. Physical disabilities, when experienced from birth, are torturous conditions that can't be attributed to someone's or society's choices. Disabled people are proof that the most serious misfortunes happen at random, they are proof that we are all subject to the unpredictability, no matter what our choices might be. Faced with the inconvenience that disable people compel us to face, it is common that we'll treat them as if they had no deficiency at all. That is the most falsely cordial way to give vent to our desire to keep their disability out of sight. If they go to the same class or are part of our group of friends, nobody will mention the issue. Disability is there, everyone sees it but behave as they didn't. In turn, when you're not able to ignore it, the need to push it away will express itself in the desire to help the disable in overcoming it. A disabled person's parents must face this kind of situation. However, because the desire to help is a manifestation of the desire to push this situation away, and because they live side by side with the disabled, the result is the guilt feeling. And where there's guilt there is need for atonement.

This is no general rule, but many parents of disabled children seek expiation of their guilt offsetting the child's disability with excessive affection, gifts, or some other excess. Many abdicate their own life in order to dedicate to their disabled child; they abdicate their life and happiness. They don't feel entitled to be happy. But these parents won't be able to atone for their fault even with all their blood, sweat, and tears as long as the conflict that brings it forth remains active. It is the conflict between affection and the desire to move away from their loved one. But parents are not the only ones who sin by excess. At work and in social life, the disabled are treated in this same "special" way. People nourish an exaggerated, childish affection for the disabled. In their presence, people express that nervous, anxious joy, as if the slightest expression of discouragement would reveal their embarrassment. Some disabled can perceive the artificiality in the air.

I believe that no disabled person wants to be treated with excessive care. Disabled people don't want others to nullify themselves in order to help them. For some, the effusive anxiety of clumsy and nervous kindness gestures only makes them feel more different. I believe also that no disabled person wants to be treated equally, if that means that their disability will be politely ignored. In order for us to have equality, do we need to offset or disregard differences? In a mathematical equation, perhaps we would. But in human relations, equality is the product of equivalence between multiple differences.

77 – NO ARGUMENT CAN WIN AGAINST A WHIM

We idealize the irreconcilable opposition between reason and emotion. We emphasize that love does not abide to reason, and that thinking with one's head and heart are very different things. I say it is not quite so. Rationality is coherence. Thus, there is nothing more rational than the most sublime emotions. Love, when devoid of attachment and selfishness is the most rational of all emotions, and therefore the best guide to behave coherently. An emotion is rational to the extent that one can no longer logically defend it and justify it to oneself and to others. The difficulty may lie in immaturity. In an argument with someone, immaturity complicates the rational formulation of emotions. However, some emotions are incoherent with the way we act and the way of acting that we expect from others, no matter how mature we are. Justifying them is impossible. By insistently nourishing them, we become whimsical. And since it's impossible to rationally justify a whim, it is also impossible for just anyone to dissuade us with their logical arguments.

138

Some fears, jealousy, and desires are contrary to what we know to be consistent with what we should do or think; fears, jealousy, and desires that we know as childish and unjustifiable because we can't justify them even to ourselves. But these are fears, jealousy, and desires that oppose our attempts to dissuade them with reason. It's as if we would shout: "I know that it makes no sense for me to feel this way or want things that way, but I do feel it and I do want it!". And this shout also echoes in the ears of those whose throats we want to force down our irrationality. The whimsical only impose themselves onto those who they know are sensitive to their demands. They know the others' weaknesses and deduce how that other will react to their tantrums. Since they can't defend themselves rationally, they impose themselves by manipulation, demonstrating better experience in human behavior than any psychologist. Whimsical people might not know how to verbalize or theoretically formulate their knowledge, but are able to sense other people's weaknesses as if they possessed a sixth sense, knowing the right moment to use it for their own benefit. They know how to communicate well with both body and speech, choosing precisely each expression; and when they decides to speak, they choose the right tone and words.

Using reason to argue with whimsical people is a mistake. The basis of their whim is not rational, so their answers will be irrational. Falling in their traps of irrationality is to let oneself be involved in it and lose the war. Their irrationality is not chaotic and meaningless. Rather, it is ingenious and treacherous. Whimsical individuals invent guilty ones, problems, barriers, difficulties and moralism to justify themselves. They use the actions and feelings of others against them, and leave everyone open-mouthed. It is impressive how words that are so unrealistic can make so much sense, as if the total lack of coherence between speech and actions could become firm and consistent only with the right choice of words, tone, and expressions. Sometimes there is no appropriate response. When the lack of logic is so logically overwhelming, we have no choice but to shut up and consent. At times like this, emotions really speak louder than reason.

There is nothing more personal and subjective than feelings. And nothing is more difficult to understand and control than an affection, a fear, a desire. Our innermost essence is, at the same time, unknown enough to control us as if we were possessed by it. It is sufficiently independent of our will so that we won't feel responsible for it. What seems paradoxical is explained by the nature of our identity. By taking a nationality, a name, a profession, we become identical to the people and the world we identify with. By taking an individuality, we become different from them. We are identical to the world and to people who differ from us. Therefore, in our identity, we differ from ourselves; we are our own other. Thus, the affective tone of our relations bears this ambivalence: emotions are personal and express our identity while expressing the other in us. The Self feels dominated, controlled, hostage of its feelings as if someone else controlled it from the inside.

If the Self is its own other, it is conscious of itself as the other. Being conscious of itself as another, it is unconscious of itself. Conscious that it loves, fears, and desires, the Self is unaware of itself. It loves, fears, and wishes because it is not aware of its identity with the other beloved, feared, and desired. And it falls into the traps of unconsciousness when identifies in the other the causes of its emotions. What is love but the sense of identity with what is different? If the other becomes identical to the Self the difference lies in the Self, not in the other. What is fear but the instability of our identity with each other? If the Self's identity is shaky, instability resides in it, not in the other. What is desire but the identity with the other which we lack? If the Self is identical to what it lacks, the lack resides inside itself, not in the other. To search in the other for the cause of our emotions is to give up all possible control over them, it is to fall into Morpheus' arms, to dive into unconsciousness and to surrender to the excesses of the other that resides in us.

If the other in us subjugates us, how can we know it and control it without contacting the other existing outside us? How can we understand love without relating to those we love? How can we overcome fear without confronting those we fear? How do we let go of desire without experiencing a momentary and illusory completeness of its realization? If the cause of the feelings lies in us, the vivid experience of emotions occurs in the contact with each other. By the contact with each other we obtain access to the dark side of our identity. The danger lies in the possibility of that access might make it even darker, and we'll believe there is no life in the absence of the other. Driven by this illusion, we become dependent on the other we love and avoid those who bother us. It's difficult to find our balance when the vivid experience of emotions occurs only in the contact with the other outside, but the solutions to our conflicts depends on this encounter.

79 – WHY DOES TIME SEEM TO FLY AFTER WE GROW UP?

Life goes by faster once we reach a certain age. When I was a child, a whole life could be lived within a day. The year-end holidays lasted forever, and the time between one Christmas and another was huge. Currently, all the adults in large urban centers complain that a year seems to last only a few months, the week barely begins and quickly comes to its end, and that life has escaped through their fingers. There is always an explanation on the tip of the tongue. The most common explanations are the routine and the information overload. It seems that the more automated and repetitive life becomes, the faster it goes by, and that the greater the amount of information assimilated during the day, the shorter the day seems to get. However, the routine has never been a problem for rural men, for example, who wake up at the same time and perform the same tasks daily. For them, time moves slowly. And the amount of information a child assimilates is much larger than that assimilated by adults. For children, everything is new. They are curious and want to know everything. A less common explanation is the lack of interest. Some say we are less interested in what we do, and therefore we are more easily bored. However, when interested in a film, for example, time also

141

appears to fly. Apparently, none of these theories solves the mystery.

The lack of interest in daily chores doesn't really explain why life seems to go by faster once we've grown. But perhaps this theory points the right way. On the one hand, life is increasingly uninteresting; on the other hand, people seem to be increasingly involved with issues and problems. They worry about everything and always have too much on their heads. It seems contradictory that people uninterested in life have so many concerns and are constantly entertained by projects and businesses. However, maybe they need so many projects and businesses because their lives are uninteresting. Life happens in the present, with what we have and who we are and it seems that, when we're raised in large cities, what we have and who we are is precisely what's uninteresting. It takes a great deal of imagination, dreams, projects, and problems so that this becomes livable. Routine and automation accelerate the passing of time because we never keep our minds in what we do. Our thoughts are always in a future that never comes, and in a past that could have been but wasn't. We think about the consequences, the products, the outcome of our routine actions... we never entertain ourselves with now. Rural men, in turn, aim not to be or to have anything other than they already are and have. They occupy themselves with what they are doing now. Their routine is always the same, and they already live it automatically, but their thoughts are where they are. Children assimilating information are also dealing with the present. What they learn is meaningful because of today, not tomorrow. We, adults, seek information because of what it can be worth in the future. The present only matters as a harbinger of a future of unsatisfying gains. And the movie that captures our attention only holds us because it opens the possibility that we might be able to shut off completely from what's around us. Entertained by a movie, we travel through the past that might have been and the future that will never be. Everything is more important than now.

To grow up is to drag behind us a past that never passes and to pursue a future that never comes; it is to abandon the present in order to live in a time that will never come to be because it has already ceased to be. Time only passes in the present. Therefore, to not live the present is to not live the passing of time and to start counting the passing of days, weeks, years. Life only goes by fast when we fail to live it and to live it, one needs to carry less baggage from the past and develop less projects for the future. One must, in short, give up the illusion that life is the realization of a huge project and learn how to realize it in the unpretentious meaninglessness of the present. And maybe that's too much to ask of those who are born and spend all life poisoned by the spirit of entrepreneurship and by the ideals of development and progress of the great urban centers.

80 – ANXIETY: THE ENEMY OF MINE

Anxiety resembles fear, but differs from it. While fear is the usual reaction to threats in real-time, anxiety is the fear that accompanies us even after the threat has passed, and that we experience in advance before it arrives. Those who are at a risk of dying in wars, robberies or kidnappings carry the threat with them and may have anxiety attacks for some time. Because the threat is never external. It's not the world that threatens us, but our frailty. So when a traumatic experience requires the recognition of how fragile we are, the fear of being hurt makes us sensitive to the touch of a feather. But the anxiety that harshly castigates our modern times has no origin in physical threat experiences. However, the threat that taunts us may seem worse than a death threat. It is the threat of losing our own self-worth and seeing our self-image deprived. In the jungle where our ancestors lived, physical threat was constant; in the concrete jungle in which we live, threats to the Self are constant. Soldiers who return from the war or accident survivors discover their physical frailty; we who live in the big city of modern times, we discover the fragility of our ego little by little. The possibility of success and failure lurks around every corner. Life is a constant loss and gain of self-worth. We go from hell to heaven and vice-versa within a minute. We're always proving something to someone; we fight to win our status and preserve it every day; we are under constant evaluation. We can't even escape the mishaps of this jungle inside our homes; in fact, the biggest threat often comes from there. There are so many hazards, so great is the weakness of our Self!

Nevertheless, being in contact with fragility doesn't justify anxiety. The men of the jungle knew themselves as fragile, but it didn't bother them. Living and dying were part of the game, and they accepted death when it came. We're not prepared to accept the death of the body and neither the death of our vanity. We're educated to be winners, beautiful, strong, fighters. Defeat and failure are presented in a poetic way to encourage us to not ever accept them. We're anxious not to accept the weakness that is so ours. Thus, it becomes an enemy with which we can't help but fighting and when the threat is installed from the inside, we see it all around. We live it in the present, whine it in the past and project it in the future suffering in advance for something that threats our vanity, exclusively.

The anxiety of modern times also brought anguish to the surface. While those dominated by anxiety believe they can – or must – overcome their fragility, the anguished accept defeat. In anguish, they recognize the invincibility of fragility. Against this recognition, we react with anxiety. Anxiety is the denial of reality triggered by anguish. However, despite its defeatist sense, the contact with anguish can mature and eliminate anxiety. We must consider this maturing in an affectionate way. We need to discuss it more openly, because collective anxiety is out of control. While most still channels it in work goals, in their search for the perfect love relationship, the perfect body, in consumerism, in alcohol, in food and in religion, there's a considerable number of people who have already been anesthetized to the effects of these loopholes, and are yielding to panic or depression. Only those who don't accept their own fragility with serenity become weak.

Relationship is communication. Thus, destroying the communication is to destroy the relationship. Those who want to relate want to communicate, and vice versa. Relationships develop with the improvement of communication. Improving communication is to develop the freedom to say what you feel and what you think. This freedom is rooted in the ability to listen to what the other feels and thinks. The inability to hear conditions one's need to impose himself. Those who don't listen to what others have to say about how they feel and what they think impose on others their own thoughts and feelings. And imposition nips in the bud the other's initiative to respond with what he feels and thinks. Only those who see the feelings and thoughts of others as threat to their position need to impose themselves. And those who feel threatened react with anger.

The yelling, threats, and blackmail are among the reactions of those who are unwilling to listen and wish only to impose themselves. People who react this way don't want to develop communication; they want to cut it as soon as possible and have the final word. The final word must be theirs, so they need to guard themselves against replicas. This creates an environment that is inappropriate for communication. The yelling, threats and blackmail don't draw their strength from arguments, but from our discouragement to continue arguing with those who don't want to hear any argument. They draw their strength from the frustration of receiving only hostile responses when talking about our feelings and thoughts; yet, they draw their strength from the resignation of those who have learned that it's useless to argue with those who are willing to impose. Through using that strength, the intolerant protect themselves against replicas.

This tactic has two possible outcomes: it can motivate the interlocutor to use the same strength or it can make him even more silent. In the first case, the relationship becomes a war between deaf people. No one listens to anyone. Each one wants to impose on the other. This war can last a long time, with no winner, as long as the two parties are on an equal footing. But if there's an asymmetrical power relationship between those involved, the rope will break on the weaker side and, when it does, it breaks because

145

the winner's strength wasn't restricted to yelling, threats, and blackmail, but benefited from restriction and punishment. So it is common that, in asymmetrical power relations, the weakest party learn to protect himself in the silence. Silence is also the option of those who understand from the beginning the lack of purpose in using this strength and don't wish to go through the arduous and exhausting learning of seeing the rope always breaking on their side. Because even when forces are matched, when the cord breaks, it breaks on both sides, although some proclaim themselves to be the winners.

When both sides yell, there is no relationship. When some yell and others learn to silence, either. And the situation can reach the height of the irrational if the one who yells accuse the one who silences of destroying the relationship by refusing to dialogue. For those who wish to impose don't necessarily expect silence as a response; they expect a "Yes, sir (or yes, ma'am). You are right". Silence is also threatening for those who wish to impose themselves. There is no bigger threat for those who fear other people's feelings and thoughts than not knowing what is going on in their head and in their heart. The strength of silence can be unbearable. Yelling can be overcome with yelling, and the winner will be the one who shouts louder. Threats and blackmail can be overcome with threats and blackmail, and the winner will be whoever is able to cause more fear. Now, what can overcome another person's silence? How can we overcome the strength of those who respond to yelling, threats, and blackmail with silent resistance? But even the silent resistance cannot establish relationships, and the silent resistant also has to live with the sad absence of a relationship.

82 – WHY IS IT SO HARD TO LOVE WITHOUT EXPECTATIONS?

Much is preached about practicing the love that expects nothing in return. If it were easy, people wouldn't insist so much on it. It's not easy to practice love without expectations. The nature of love can explain that. Love is only fulfilling when there is reciprocity.

Therefore, not expecting reciprocity is contrary to love. Love happens when we establish the identity with another. The other is only an other because he is different from us. In identifying, we become identical to who's different, and our identity becomes different from ourselves. In practice, the identity is lost. But its loss doesn't mean it disappears. We know very well where it is. In identifying with another person, he becomes our identity. This is expressed when you feel you're giving yourself to the other. And the sense of giving remains even in the absence of effective actions in behalf of the other. Feeling is giving already. The simple feeling of identifying with the other is already giving yourself to him. We donate our identity to the other; but the identity donated never becomes hiss; it remains the identity of whoever donated. The other becomes the bearer of an identity he's been given, and that identity is mine. Consequently, the other becomes mine.

Nothing is more valuable than our identity. Without it, we are not. Our being is expressed in it. However, in identifying with itself, the Self is aware of the other as an other or, depending on the situation, as an object. An object he uses at will. Love alters that. In love, the other ceases to be just an other to become the bearer of a being who loves him, and this means a lot. If the lover's being lies within the other, what is left for the lover? He can only express the void of someone who gave himself to another, and this emptiness needs compensation. If the lover's emptiness is not compensated, he feels as if he could no longer be; as if the identity given to the other had been really lost and could no longer be found. Compensation occurs when the other reciprocates this love. This mutuality experience means great achievement, for the identity with the other would never be realized as such if he didn't recognize it as real. If my identity is the other, the other's identity has to be my Self and my Self only becomes the identity of the other if the other recognizes it that way. If the other who expresses my identity also expresses his identity in me, he ceases to be the difference that denies me and becomes the difference in me that I realize as identical to myself. The other ceases to be an other to become mine, and I cease being me to become hiss.

147

Love needs reciprocity. It expresses our most humanly noble side and the most humanly fragile. However, its noble side brings us to another form of love, without mutuality. Loving without expectations is an existential necessity, for the hazards of expecting are great. And loving without expecting is possible. We've all experienced it. We've all passed by a baby on the street and smiled without expecting a smile in return. Through that smile, we give ourselves in a definite way, because we keep going without looking back. If giving ourselves without expectations is possible, perhaps the lack is only experienced with incomplete love. Perhaps the love that expects nothing in return doesn't make us feel in need of love, and perhaps we are much more prepared to practice this love than we give ourselves credit for.

83 – EXPECTATION RUINS OUR RELATIONSHIPS

The ideal is opposed to the real by definition. Ideal is what exists only as an idea, which is not yet realized. Therefore, when an ideal becomes real, their ideal existence is lost. I am not discussing if an ideal can or cannot come true. I would like to draw attention instead to the fact that the ideals are formed when knowledge is incipient. In the absence of constituted knowledge, there is the idea about that which we don't really know yet. All incipient knowledge is constituted of ideas more than facts, and the less familiar we are with the facts, the more idealized is the knowledge. If the idealization is greater when the familiarity with the facts is smaller, there is no doubt younger people idealize more. And compensating the lack of familiarity with the facts, the ideals express how facts are imagined. It will be no surprise if we find we always imagine the facts as we wish or fear.

Fears and expectations point toward the future. The future is unknown, therefore, fears and expectations are idealizations. And the contact with reality reverberates differently in fears and expectations. Reality dispels any imaginary fears. It is difficult, however, to accept the challenge to test them in reality. But the effect of reality upon expectations is different; expectations related

148

to political or social ideals are easier to preserve. However far the reality might be from them, it's possible to believe the day in which the idealized world and the idealized society will take place. And the reality that tells us otherwise will only make us more fanatical. However, it is not always possible to preserve the expectation toward others. Indeed, those who idealize society preserve their dream because they never test it. In turn, those who dream of a romantic ideal also preserve it for as long as it isn't tested. After the first frustration, the task becomes more arduous. At this point, the need for the newly acquired familiarity with the facts to take the place of ideals comes about. This process of substitution can be called maturity. In the absence of maturity, the expectations we haven't left behind become distrust and bitterness.

When we don't abandon our expectations toward others, frustrations cause mistrust and bitterness. Moreover, we preserve idealizations that don't correspond to people. And we can't give them what they need and expect from us unless we abandon our expectations and learn to really know them. By nourishing expectations about others, we form a picture of who they should be and what they should do. It is with this image that we relate, not with real people, when we mediate our relationships by expectations. Learning to know people so we can give them what they need is no guarantee that we'll receive the same in return. But it guarantees mature reactions to future frustrations. Those who know people know they really can hurt us, and they can do us well, too. Only those who don't accept the distance between real and idealized people become bitter and suspicious.

84 – HOMOSSEXUALITY AND HETEROSSEXUALITY ARE OF THE SAME NATURE

There has always been interest in finding the cause of homosexuality. The fact that the same is not true for heterosexuality intrigues me. Heterosexuality is seen naturally, and whatever is natural doesn't require a common sense explanation. Nature, however, is the object of science. Science studies natural phenomena and seeks explanations for homosexuality regarded as unnatural by common sense. Perhaps homosexuality is controversial because common sense has not yet related it to heterosexuality. If we bring homosexuality and heterosexuality close together, perhaps homosexuality will not remain so enigmatic and heterosexuality will not remain so natural.

In a practice called role reversal, the woman wears a belt with a dildo and penetrates her partner's anus. Because it is a sexual act between a man and a woman, it is considered a heterosexual sex act. But what can we say of the desire fulfilled by it? I think part of the drive that constitutes that desire is homosexual. It is a homosexual drive satisfied in a heterosexual relationship. The homosexual drive meddles in heterosexual relationships even in the most unsuspected cases. Take, for example, the common case of males attracted by women with thighs that resemble soccer player's thighs. They're women with male physical attributes, but which arouse male desire. Many make use of anabolic steroids to achieve that look. And what about men attracted to women with male personality traits? Dominant, aggressive women, women who take the initiative. And it's not just homosexuality that meddles in heterosexuality; the opposite also occurs in various shades. Just as there are men who enjoy being penetrated by women, there are those who like to be penetrated by transvestites and those who prefer to be penetrated by man with manly traits. On the other hand, there are men who like to penetrate women, men who enjoy penetrating transvestites and those men who also prefer penetrating men with manly traits. Heterosexuality and homosexuality are mixed in various shades and in both directions. Straight peoples satisfy homosexual drives in their relationships, often without realizing it. The opposite also occurs, of course.

As far as I know, there is no pure form of heterosexuality or homosexuality. We should question the nature of sexuality, including heterosexuality. Heterosexuality is a riddle as complex as homosexuality: why, after all, are heterosexuals attracted to objects different from themselves? If we understand the mystery of heterosexuality, we understand the homosexuality: Why, after all, is the homosexual attracted by the object that is identical to himself?

By understanding one thing and another, we'll be able to treat homosexuality as naturally as we treat heterosexuality. We should, however, consider both as enigmatic in the first place.

85 – WHY DO WE LIVE IN INSECURITY?

Insecurity is one of those little words in the psychological vocabulary whose broad meaning can result in the lack of meaning. Because insecurity is everywhere. Everything can be explained by some form of insecurity, and we all live with it. A feeling so universal and so present shouldn't be so little understood. However, the closest things are the most difficult to put into perspective. Insecurity is inconsistency; the inconsistent is unstable because it lacks coherence. We are insecure because we're incoherent. We identify with each other to form our individuality. Our individuality is established in the identity with each other. Thus, the individuated personality is that which realizes its identity with the other. This incoherence is our nature. Knowing insecurity is knowing the incoherence of the security we always sought. Those who become aware of their own insecurity acknowledge having vainly sought for security in other people, things, circumstances, and hopes. Then, they understand somewhat loosely that it's necessary to stop seeking security outside and find it inside. This idea is noble and praiseworthy, however, it is vague and nebulous. After all, what does it mean to search for security within myself? Does it mean to stop searching in the places I've searched so far? Certainly! But I should cease to seek it there to start seeking where, specifically? Where is this "myself" in which I should seek the security that I lack? My "myself" is the other with whom I've established my identity.

It isn't incoherent to search for security in the other, but to not seek it in the other as a whole. Because the other is everywhere, the other is the world. However, our identification is restricted to romantic partners, children, friends, the social status we cherish, the job that sustains us, etc. We don't realize our identity with the world, but with a fraction of it. Notwithstanding, the world changes constantly, forcing us to deal with the possibility that the very small part that completes us can change, can be lost, annihilated. In the broad identity with the world, insecurity finds no room for itself. For if we suffered a loss here, we would still have myriad of means everywhere to sustain our identity.

To seek security in ourselves means to seek it in our identity. Therefore, in order for us to feel secure, we must invest in the wider realization of our identity with the world. In other words, it means to remove a portion of the importance given to the few things that complete us and distribute it to many other things so that the identity has good support. By restricting our identification to a portion of the world, everything else that is excluded acquires a threatening sense. What threatens us should also be part of identity. Insecurity fills the points of our relationship with the world where the identity that should exist hasn't been realized. Therefore, security lies in what makes us insecure; there lies the unrealized essence of identity; that's where we must turn in search of a more focused and authentic life.

86 – INNER BEAUTY DOES NOT EXIST

Beauty is a female trait. A man with feminine features is beautiful, but a woman with masculine traits is far from beautiful. Women have always been valued for their beauty. And although they still worship this value, some have felt uncomfortable over time. The feeling of having more to offer than physical beauty emerged among women; the need to be recognized and valued by different attributes arose among them. I don't know to what extent the concept of inner beauty emerged or was strengthened with the feminist spirit, but it is linked to the desire of women to free themselves from the oppression of physical beauty. Because in addition to leaving other qualities in the shade, the physical beauty empire imposes women to frame themselves into an aesthetic standard that excludes most of them. Against the requirement of being always thin, well dressed and with make-up, and against the blurring of personality in favor of the body, feminism claimed that women were as intelligent and capable as men, and that they should be valued not only by physical beauty. Without realizing it, feminism exchanged the oppression of outer beauty for the oppression of inner beauty. Where once women were striving to produce and preserve physical beauty, they saw themselves then forced to prove their intelligence and ability. And if on one hand the oppression of physical beauty left women's personality in the shadow, the oppression of inner beauty put them in a competition course with men that left aside their femininity. When the cry of equality ignores the differences rather than giving them the same value, equality becomes as oppressive as discrimination.

Inner beauty is as overwhelming as outer beauty because both impose a standard to follow. As well as the current standards of female physical beauty establish thinness as an ideal, the inner beauty standards establish intelligence, kindness, fellowship, helpfulness, empathy and the ability to understand others as the ideal of the "beautiful soul". However, beauty is not found in any of these attributes. One can be intelligent and still be despicable to us. One can also seem kind, friendly, helpful, empathetic and yet be less beautiful than someone we consider selfish, individualistic, insensitive, and useless. What makes someone's interior beautiful is affection, and affection can make beautiful everything that is contrary to beauty's formal standards. Isn't that what makes it so enigmatic? There are those who love the selfish, the individualistic, the useless, the insensitive and don't understand why they love them, believing they shouldn't, because they've adopted the standards of inner beauty. Those who adopt inner beauty standards think they can only love other who meet these standards. They believe there's no beauty outside these standards and yet they get stunned when they find beauty where, theoretically, it shouldn't be.

Inner beauty does not exist. Those who don't like anyone don't see beauty in anyone, and those who like everyone sees beauty in every face and every soul. Other people's inner beauty depends on our willingness to love them, and our inner beauty depends on others liking us. Our ability to like people increases our chances of others liking us, and what increases our chances liking other people is the ability to see similarities where there are differences. In turn, when we can dissolve the contact tension between the differences by relaxing, our ability to see similarities in differences increases. When we feel comfortable around others, they feel comfortable around us. I don't speak of forced and artificial relaxation that characterizes our social life so well; I speak of the relaxation that only the uncomplicated affection produces. We can truly say that this affection radiates its inner beauty wherever it goes.

87 – CRIMINAL LIABILITY AGE REDUCTION

Our opinions are one-sided because we choose between opposite alternatives when we should understand how they complement each other. The great difficulty of our understanding is to unify what is separated by opposition. Generally, we don't realize that. The opposition of alternatives deceives us and we choose one or the other. Psychology has an explanation for this. The identity of our Self is the world, but in consciousness prevails the distinction between us and the world. So we either allocate in the world all the guilt for who we are or we carry the guilt of the world on our shoulders, when we should understand that we are the world, and vice versa. Every identity is a two-way street: if the world is our Self, it is responsible for who we are. But if our Self is the world, the responsibility for who we are is ours. The responsibility of the world doesn't negate ours, and vice versa. Consequently, the world in which we are born and live can explain our actions, but never justify them.

I still haven't found an intelligent opinion on the issue of reducing the criminal liability age. Because those discussing it either claim that teenagers are responsible for what they do or claim that this is a social issue rather than a human issue. Those supporting the teenagers' liability have the reactionary attitude as their weakness and those who defend social causality have as their weakness the romanticism of believing that men are born good but are later corrupted by the environment. On the one hand it is

154

undeniable that social factors increase the possibility of a teenager choosing for a criminal life, but it is also true that worldwide children and teenagers of middle and upper class, with no history of abuse, commit crimes, from small felonies to murder. Thus, it's not worth wasting time discussing whether it is a human or social issue. It is a human and social issue. What we can't, under any circumstances, do is to use the social factor to remove the individual's responsibility and use the individual's responsibility to turn a blind eye to the social problem. Among those who are against the reduction of criminal liability age, perhaps the most common opinion is that the prison system has no means to recover criminals, and that they come out of prison worse than they entered. But can structural problems in prisons justify impunity? Another point widely raised is that imprisonment doesn't reduce crime. Do these people mean then that the best alternative is to extinguish the prison system and to grant freedom to criminals?

The social factor must be taken into account, as well as the precariousness of our prison system. But none of this can be used to nullify the responsibility of a child or teenager who commits a crime. A child or teenager who commit minor crimes with no serious or permanent consequences for third parties must be sheltered by the state, especially if they live in social risk conditions. They should receive a lenient sentence to be served in institutions that aim for re-education. Even though the individual's liability can't be denied, it is the responsibility of the state that should be considered in this case. But the child or teenager who commits serious crimes such as murder cannot live in impunity, no matter the social risk conditions they live in and how precarious the prison system is. Even if society's responsibility can't be denied, it is the individual's liability that must be taken into account in this case. Without respect for other people's lives there is no possible society. Attacks on life, especially those with cruelty cannot be justified by social factors. Those who transfer a killer's responsibility to the state or society destroy the notion of responsibility, for the state's or society's responsibility belongs to everyone and no one. Who is the State? Who is the society, blamed

155

for everything? Are the politicians to blame? Each politician is also just one individual among all the others. Without the principle that we are responsible for what we do, there is no possible ethics. We can't expect a response from a criminal teenager nor from the corrupt politician. We're all nothing more than a product of the environment in which we live. We must strive to improve the prison system so that it will enable the recovery of criminals, but we can't use its precariousness or social risk factors to justify the impunity and the objectification that exempts people of what they do.

88 – THE WORST PART OF SUFFERING IS LONELINESS

What is suffering? Suffering is any state of isolation from the world. It is the absence of a bridge that connects us to the world. We suffer for having lost or for having never possessed that which realizes our identity, and we suffer for the fear of something like that happening. In both cases, it's as if the world had suddenly turned its back on us; it's as if it had left us talking to ourselves and become deaf to our pleas. Suddenly, it's as if there were no life on the outside. And since there is no life outside, there is no life inside. The feeling of being isolated from the world is loneliness. So every suffering is a form of loneliness. While loneliness is strictly the demand for company, suffering, in a general sense, is the feeling of having been left talking to oneself; the feeling that the world no longer pays attention to what we feel and what we have to complain about.

If all suffering is loneliness, the feeling that we suffer while being surrounded by people is paradoxical. It's like being thirsty and yet unable to drink water or to drink water and still be thirsty. Being around people and still feel isolated is suffocating. If the bridge that connects us to the world still keeps us away from it, the problem seems insoluble, and anguish suffocates us. Anguish suffocates because even in the face of a world that seems deaf to what we have to say, there's no alternative but to try to talk to it. And the desire to speak to a world that seems insensitive to our words makes the words vanish. Therefore, the hardest thing in anguish is to find the right words and, not finding the right words, we don't know where to start.

Anguish puts us in an impasse: we need to speak to a world that, in our view, doesn't listen to us. How can we dialogue with it? If people are the connection with the world, we need to talk to people. But no one listen to us, including ourselves. Isolated from the world, we're isolated from ourselves. Therefore we are the first to become deaf to our own pleas. In order for us to hear what we have to say, we need someone to listen to us. But if we are unable to listen to what we say, we believe that no one else can.

In turn, however, we need to believe that someone will listen to us, for this is our only possibility to connect to the world. Between the belief that no one can listen to us and the belief that someone could, we react in two opposite ways, depending on our temper. There are those who isolate themselves in silence, hoping their silent cry will be heard; and there are those who exhaust themselves in verbiage, hoping their chatter will allow them to hear their own silence. Those who suffer and isolate themselves in silence believe to be the only ones able to understand themselves, but expect their silence can speak to the world and be understood by all. Those who suffer and feel the need to speak believe that others can listen to them and understand them, but expect to find in chattering the silence that gives it meaning.

If we believe we're misunderstood by the world, we will seek in vain to understand ourselves in silence. If we believe that we are unable to understand ourselves, we will seek in vain to make ourselves understood in chattering. Our identity is the world. Isolated from the world, we're isolated from ourselves, and vice versa. Our understanding of ourselves depends on our communion with the world, and our communion with the world depends on the ability to understand ourselves. Where one lacks the understanding of oneself, one lacks communion with the world, which is filled with suffering; and where one lacks communion with the world, one is dominated by loneliness. Loneliness is the worst part of suffering. In the loneliness of suffering, we suffer from shortness of breath in the open. Wise

157

Orientals prescribe breathing exercises to overcome suffering. It is likely that we suffer just because we don't know how to breathe properly.

89 – THE BONDS OF THE PAST DO NOT EXIST

The past seems to keep us tied up. Our present problems seem to be tied to a past that unfolded in numerous processes until it led to the current state of affairs. When we think back, we visualize the past as a line that starts in the present and goes all the way through the years we've lived. Along that line, we place a series of events with which we didn't deal properly on their own time, and whose negative effects have been accumulating to form the weight we carry on our backs today. And so we think: if present problems are the effect of several cumulative processes of the past, then they can only be solved at a later time along which everything that got curled up can unfold. If we imagine the past as the time over which we got caught up in problems, we will also imagine the future as the time required for us to untie ourselves. Thus, the present is crushed between a troubled past and a painful future of adjustments. By believing that the cause of our problems is in the past, we situate the solution in the future, and the farther into the past we situate the causes of our problems, the farther in the future we will place the solutions. It's hard not to be discouraged, but it's even harder to understand that this timeline is a creation of imagination.

Time can play tricks on us when we imagine it as a line or a road. If we imagine temporal extension as a line curled up in us, we'll imagine that a similar temporal extension is needed so we can be uncurled. If we imagine time as a long road that led us down the wrong path, we'll imagine the need to walk a similar distance so we can go back and take the right path. But time is nothing like that. Past and future do not exist; the past no longer exists and the future doesn't exist yet. Our problems are current. Even if we imagine current problems as the effect of past problems, current problems will still be present due to current circumstances. And if we imagine it's only possible to change current circumstances in the future, we'll be contradicting ourselves with words. It is obvious that these circumstances may be changed in the present, because they exist only in the present, and can be changed in the time they exist. They can't be changed in a time that doesn't yet exist – and may never come to exist.

Much of what disturbs us in the present connects to our relationships, to our professional status and even to our body image. And relationships are built over time; it takes time to establish ourselves professionally, no one loses weight or gets defined muscles overnight, and so on. If it took us some time to gain weight, we'll probably need some time to be in shape again. Many things can't be changed immediately. But every reality is a present reality, and the present is subject to current factors. If reality can't be suddenly changed, the circumstances that condition it and that preserve it in the current state can be changed immediately. If our relationships can't be changed today, our attitudes can. And even though the people with whom we relate don't change in any way, the change in our attitudes will change their meaning to us and our relationship with them. We'll cease using their actions as justification for our frustration, and we'll learn to give them the affection we've always wanted, even with the limits they impose. Changing our attitude in the workplace is also no guarantee that things will be better, but it ensures that we'll learn to suffer less from the difficulties and become more capable to resolve them. Similarly, starting a diet or starting a workout routine doesn't guarantee miraculous results, but it assures us the feeling to be doing everything in our power to be at peace with our own bodies, which changes our self-esteem, far more important than the body self-image.

Part of reality can't be changed in the blink of an eye and some can't be changed at all, but subjective attitudes that influence anxiety can be changed immediately, because the bonds of the past do not exist. This doesn't mean anxiety will be eliminated immediately. It means that if the subjective attitudes that condition it are changed, it will certainly come to its end. It's just a matter of time...

159

We feel threatened when our emotional demands are not attended to. The Self is formed through personal relationships; it's through the identification with others that our identity is formed. Thus, emotional frustrations are threats to our identity. All frustration is emotional and all dissatisfaction is frustration, including hunger. Therefore, threats to organic survival are also frustrations, and threaten the Self. Small children have no notion of what can threaten their lives. For them, hunger is the absence of a nutritional relationship with the other. Therefore, a child who angrily cries of hunger is protesting against the conditions of their emotional relationships.

Frustration is the cause of anger. Anger protests against the precarious state of affection, and its goal is to improve it. That is precisely what makes it so ineffective, because it pushes people away rather than bringing them closer. Anger worsens the state of affairs against which it protests, and no behavior will remain unchanged when its goal is to constantly frustrated. The angry demonstrations tend to wilt after successive and constant negative consequences. Gradually, we give up trying to reach out to others with our anger. I would like to say that this giving up occurs as we learn more effective ways to get closer. However, the suppression of angry demonstrations usually means settling for unsatisfactory relationships. Not expressing anger may be a sign of maturity, but it also means we've ceased fighting for the best. Nevertheless, it doesn't mean we no longer wish for the best. Angry demonstrations can be suppressed; not anger. Inside, frustration remains and anger, too. Anger manifestation is no longer explicit, that's all. It implodes within. The negative consequences of anger teach us that swallowing our anger is more convenient. It may not help much in the search for desired relationships, but it doesn't threat the little we have, and amid the difficulty of getting the best, we settle in preserving what we have.

Even though we're dissatisfied with our relations, we fear we'll worsen them if we let our anger out. So the anger that was once a reaction to the threat becomes a threat itself. We then start fearing our anger expressions and avoiding any situation that displeases us. For that, we distance ourselves even more from those who we'd like to come closer to. We sink deeper into our conformism, and conformism numbs us until we forget that we've once desired the best. We forget, moreover, that we still wish for the best. Even the most outgoing people develop this conformism. In a sense, becoming adults and reaching maturity is to develop it. Mitigating conformism requires assessing the demands addressed to others; it requires awareness that frustration's threats are illusory; awareness that our Self withstands care denials to even the most severe demands. Mitigating conformism and rescuing the living sense of affection requires us to, finally, embrace the world's denials without fear to turn threatening anger into the warm enthusiasm of expanding affection.

91 – WE ALL CARE ABOUT WHAT OTHERS THINK

Who cares about what others think? We all do. There are those who deny it and those who accept it, those who ignore other people's opinions and those who take it too seriously. But we all care about what others think. And among us, the ones who care the most are precisely those who insist on shouting to the world they do not care, because what could be the purpose of saying they don't care except for convincing others? And why try to convince others if we don't care about what they think? Greater than the fear of what others think about us is the fear of having them realize that their opinion has affected us. That explains why some like to show indifference or even disdain for other people's opinions. They say "words will never hurt me", or "low blows don't strike me" but they do. And a good learner realizes that the effort to keep the chin always high indicates that "low blows" actually can strikes us, in full.

The alleged indifference toward other people's opinions is a manifestation of pride. A proud person inflates the value he attributes to himself. Unable to increase his own value with the value he finds within, he removes the value of others and implants it in himself. He is also the one who attributes value to others, without realizing it. For a proud person, the value of others is real and is part of who they are. Therefore, removing the value of others and implanting it in his own Self is an artificial operation that doesn't even convince him. Deep down, he continues believing that the value of others is real, and that his own value is a farce created by himself. What is the intent of this farce? It's to convince others that he believes in his own value. If others believe that the proud is convinced of his self-worth, they will also believe that he doesn't care about what they think of him. The proud person's greatest desire is to pass the impression of not caring about what others think. Thus, demonstrating weakness to others' opinions is his greatest fear.

But it is precisely the fear of showing weakness to others' opinions that makes someone actually fragile to what others think. If there's no fear of showing weakness, weakness doesn't exist. And if weakness doesn't exist, you can't show it. What appears instead is sensitivity, mature and safe, to what others say. When sensitivity gets mixed with fragility, our attitude toward what others think can range from indifference to hysteria, two extremes of manifested pride. But when sensitivity is expressed without fragility, we don't deny the effect of other people's words upon us: we calmly give them feedback, and instead of fragility we pass on a noble image. Fortitude and self-worth are not the product of indifference, but the ability to calmly tell others how their actions and words affected us. In serenity lies self-security, so pursued by the proud. However, whereas the proud denies the importance and the effect of other peoples' words about himself, security lies in accepting such importance and in communicating it with serenity to whom it may be necessary. What distinguishes frail people from self-assured people, proud from serene, those with high self-esteem from those with low self-esteem is not the fact that they do or don't care about what others think. We all care about what

162

others think, but those who reconcile their own self-worth with the importance given to what others think are able to peacefully deal with others' opinions; and those who put their own value in conflict with the importance given to the opinions of others will only react to it in a proud way.

92 – WE STOP RELATING TO OTHERS WHEN WE START DREAMING

A successful career, lots of money, the fairy tale, the perfect body. These are the great dreams that move most of us; dreams that weren't there during childhood. In a way, to grow up is to dive headfirst into our dreams, and it is convenient to put them first in the day's to do list, because it is easy to find in them a meaning for life. However, to seek for the meaning of life in dreams, although magnificent dreams, is to seek for it outside the present reality, in possibilities that point to the future. When we identify many opportunities for personal fulfillment in the present, we are filled with enthusiasm, but when we don't identify any possibility we surrender to melancholy and depression. However, a present of possibilities is as empty as a present devoid of possibilities. The enthusiasm is what prevents us from perceiving that.

When we make a dream come true, we need to quickly start pursuing another. Achievement is gratifying, but doesn't meet our expectations. Those who fulfill the dream of getting married soon begin to dreaming of children. If the children don't come, the goals are directed to a professional life. Those who dedicate to their professional lives for a long time dream of starting a family, but those who are already married, have seen their children grow up and have already built their career face the emptiness of the present. For if the present is evaluated by its possibilities, it becomes empty when there are no more dreams to fulfill, despite the beautiful memories of the past.

As we begin to dream big, we lose the ability to make and keep friends. Most friendships are built during childhood and teenage years. But the difficulty in making friends in adulthood is not

163

commonly related to the dawn of big dreams. In childhood and adolescence, before we start dreaming big, it is the coexistence with others that makes the present vivid, and making friends is our main goal. We get excited with the possibilities that point to a very short-term future such as the next weekend or vacation approaching, excited to interact with those of our age. However, when we start dreaming big, we begin to walk alone, in an individualistic journey toward a final line that never comes. People who cross our path are temporary acquaintances. It's not worth getting attached to them. Our great personal dreams are more important than establishing bonds, and our acquaintances are also pursuing their own dreams. They participate in our daily lives for a short period of time but we know that sooner or later they will follow their path. The friendships we made in childhood and adolescence become contact in our social networks. Many of them are now married, such as many of us. They don't interrupt the daily rush to see old friends and neither do we. We all just keep the promise of meeting someday.

As we chase our dreams, people come and go from our lives, and we see life pass by. Even though we dream with finding love and having children, the dream only makes sense because we've ceased relating to those who are present. Children and loving partners are idealized and ideal people only gain importance when we fail to relate to real people. Thus, it is also by ceasing to connect to people that the present is only lived in view of the possibilities, condemning us to an artificial life that will charge its price when there are no more dreams to fulfill. What keeps the present vivid is supporting others, establishing bonds and making exchanges, as if nothing else mattered. That's what makes childhood and adolescent memories so sweet. That's what we lose when we become adults.

93 – THE FUTILITIES OF THE SMILE

Babies start to smile when their relationships with their parents become significant. The faces that make them smile and that are part of many pleasant past experiences are also confirmed as pleasant in the present by the smile itself. In this sense, a baby's smile is a welcome card. The person being smiled to is informed that the baby is open to relate to him. The smile's general meaning is openness. It indicates that we're open to the world and that, conversely, we feel it open to us. At least that's the meaning of a smile while we're still authentic, while we're children. As we grow older and learn to relate socially, the scenario changes. For a child, the concept of social relations doesn't make sense. Children are nice to others when they open up to them, and unpleasant in the opposite case. The need to always be nice doesn't make sense to them. However, as we become socialized men and women, the meaning of the smile is reversed. We learn to smile not to express openness, but to close within us what we don't want to expose. Smiling becomes a mask. The opening it symbolizes is merely formal. At best, those who smile in a social environment are prepared to be kind and considerate, and their kindness works as a barricade where they study the terrain to see how far they can go, if they have any interest in moving forward whatsoever. At worst, when there is no interest in moving forward in the relationship, smiling turns people away as gently as possible.

Smiling is addictive because it is convenient. When we learn to smile to close ourselves and keep others away, we create a comfortable distance from them. The smile keeps people away, but not far enough to cause discomfort. We smile to inform them we are still willing to be kind to them, even though we keep them away. The smile is like a consolation prize distributed to and received from everyone. And those who get used to it give up fighting for the champion's trophy, because the struggle for the top prize brings hazards we're not willing to face. Opening up to others leaves us vulnerable. We learn that lesson gradually, and a baby hasn't learned yet. When we learn that opening leaves us vulnerable but scowling only brings hostilities, we smile even though we're locked inside. And by smiling while locked inside, we implicitly accept that people will remain closed to us, as long as they're no too closed. We agree with the rules of the game.

165

The world would be different if smiles could preserve in adulthood the same opening of when we smiled for the first time. The world would be different if we smiled only from affection, and if the smile lead us to laughs of camaraderie, tenderness, and complicity, where there is intimacy. However, the adult smile is a mask of a locked inner side, where affection is entrenched. Why do we need to smile in order to get closer if a smile is the expression of proximity? How can we be authentic in a smile that is given from a distance? If there's already no proximity in the smile, it won't bring us any closer to others. Perhaps, we should "have only two hands and the feeling of the whole world" like a Brazilian poet once wrote, and thus we would open up to the wind, the sun, other people. That's not the feeling that overflows every time formality and habit require us to smile in photos. That's not the feeling that moves our laughter and smiles in social life. The world belongs to those who adopt the futility as a rule. Those who stubbornly entangle in authenticity have a tough road ahead.

94 – NO ONE PREPARES IN ADVANCE FOR LIFE

Some things we are only prepared to do as age comes. Driving, working, getting involved in a love relationship are examples. No matter how mature a child is and how prepared he is in other things: some businesses require preparation that only age provides. Most of us had to wait for the right age to do grown-up things. Our parents and educators explained that we weren't ready yet, and they were right. However, this education suitable for children can block us as we become adults. It seems that even after we've grown we tell ourselves we have to wait a little longer to do certain things. When we don't feel prepared for something, we believe that the solution is to wait for the right time, a time when preparation finally arrives. The philosophy of waiting for the right moment, giving ourselves more time to prepare should be abandoned when we leave behind the teenage years and enter adulthood. Whereas it is necessary to wait a few more years for certain activities when we're children, as adults waiting is waste of time. Whereas we believe as children that age will bring us the maturity required to enter certain businesses, as adults the maturity obtained in waiting only makes us more inexperienced rather than more mature. Whereas in childhood and adolescence preparation comes with time, in adulthood delegating preparation to time is to wait for it in vain. When we become adults, preparation is never given in advance. It is built as we live.

We usually think that being prepared means having no fear. That is a mistake. There will always be fear. Fear will accompany us until our last day. In this sense, even children and adolescents don't receive preparation in advance for anything. In fact, they don't receive preparation; they receive responsibility. Age doesn't make them prepared, it enables them to answer for what they do. Therefore, even they – or especially they – are forced to face their fears when life requires them to participate in life's business. And if they were to wait for the fear to go away, they would never take the first step. Being prepared is not being fearless. We prepare ourselves to accept the possibility of fears coming true. We do not cease to fear the worst; just calmly accept the possibility that the worst can happen. Being prepared isn't being sure that everything will be alright, it isn't having exuberant confidence in success. No one's sure of the future. Confidence in success is a farce of self-deception and only those unable to accept life's possible moves need the ways of self-deception. Confident people are not those who believe in success; confident people accept the possibility of failure. Because failure always exists as a possibility, as well as success. Those who accept the possibility that the worst can happen still fear it, but they're prepared to face it if it comes.

Fear doesn't make us unprepared, panic does. Fear can be faced, and we face it with resignation that things may occur differently from what we've desired. Panic, in turn, springs from the intolerance toward the worst possibilities. When we are aware that the worst can happen we experience actual fear. Panic is when we fear that awareness. Panic is fearing fear; it is fear to power of fear. Those who panic experience the fear of being afraid. They don't accept the possibility that the worst can happen, they don't accept the possibility of fearing the prospect of the worst. In short, those

167

overwhelmed by panic are the most addicted to the childhood education. They believed better than anyone that the preparation for life should come in advance, that preparation comes over time, with age. They haven't understood that we prepare for life as we live; the verb "to prepare" should only be conjugated in the gerund, never in the infinitive, for the preparation is never complete, it never ends. We never reach the moment when we have it entirely at hand, ready for whatever comes. Those who throw themselves forward, even though unprepared, are those really prepared for life, those who don't have preparation as a condition to live.

95 – THE IMAGINARY PRISON OF NEEDINESS

We are ashamed to talk about neediness. When people declare themselves needy, they pass on the impression that they are pouting, emotionally blackmailing others and not behaving with the expected austerity of an adult. The responses they receive to their plea, even if silent, express that criticism. Thus, people don't talk much of their own neediness, although they easily express it in their actions. Neediness is motivation for intrigues, for demands, and misunderstanding. Not to mention the feelings of jealousy, contempt, anger, love, tenderness, desire, etc. When we think about neediness, we usually make an analogy with malnutrition and imagine it as a "malnutrition of the soul". And as malnutrition is a cumulative physical condition that requires a long period of careful intake of nutrients, we imagine this shortage as a condition of the soul that is reflected in the physical body, requiring a lot of human contact of every kind, managed carefully for a long time. However, even though sunk in the depth of a historically built neediness, sometimes a simple sign, a mere look or the words of a special someone is enough to make the past meaningless and the present a warm place.

We've all been through this. Drowned in a deep and old neediness which we judge rooted and entangled, we suddenly see it revealed in all its ephemerality and disappearing as if by magic.

However, the magic doesn't last more than an instant. The duration of a kindly gesture, for instance. The heat awakened cools shortly after so we return to the cold vastness of the imagination where neediness is a monster consuming us. It is as if the heat of moment was a brief commercial break of the main show, and after watching it so many times, we know the breaks don't last long and it's no use getting excited about them. We no longer allow fantasy to evade reality. However, we may be confusing fantasy for reality and reality for fantasy. Perhaps the neediness show that is so long, so old and so often replayed, is fantasy itself.

It is possible that the moments of warmth seem so quick because we judge them for the duration of the event that triggered it. The impression of a gesture, for example, goes away. Depending on the gesture, it can last long, but it always goes away. And when the meaning of a gesture drops in an ocean of doubts, the impression goes even faster. We wonder if it really meant what we wanted it to. Well, the meaning of the gesture wouldn't be so important if, instead of valuing the gesture, we'd value the warmth that woke us up and the greater openness to the world provided. The warmth of the moment makes us lighter and open to others; people become less stern and more open to us; and in this state of affairs, there is no neediness. This openness is real, and the world's response to it also. However, we forget to preserve the warmth once aroused. The arousing is involuntary, but preserving the warmth in our hearts is an act of will. We voluntarily allow the heart to cool down and the openness to diminish. We demand its maintenance of others when it is our responsibility. By neglecting our duty, we return to the cold, imaginary prison of neediness as if it were real and we also return to the illusory warmth, without noticing that we imprison ourselves in our own lack of initiative. I believe this intuition is implicit in our reproach to those who openly declare their own neediness. This doesn't mean reproach is justified. Still, we need to think more about the fictional side of neediness and the way we let ourselves be imprisoned by it.

Sometimes we have the feeling we're living surrounded by well-resolved people, with good self-esteem, and free from the insecurities we endure. Sometimes we have the feeling of we're living in a world of people who are indifferent to what surrounds them, happy with what they possess, and we feel that the need to compare ourselves to others is only ours. It's as if we were the only needy ones, the only ones who need attention, the only ones suffering the bitterness of feeling left out. By feeling this way, we nurture a widespread resentment that motivates us to return to the world the same indifference and detachment that we judge we receive from it. But do we realize that? In fact, we rarely do. When we adopt the attitude of indifference to return to people the indifference with which, in our view, they treat us, it's as if we were wearing a mask. We wear the mask of indifference. However, we unconsciously believe that others can see beneath it. Our deepest intention is to make them suffer what they make us suffer and that intention is motivated in the unconscious belief that they know how badly their indifference makes us feel. But just as we believe in other people's mask of indifference, they also believe in ours. And just as their mask makes us feel alone in a world of well resolved people, ours makes them feel the same. Only a few have the foresight to see beneath the mask. Most easily believe in masks of high self-esteem, happiness and security that people around them wear.

When we wear the mask of indifference, our unconscious intention is to communicate that we're hurt by the indifference of others, and we want more attention. By keeping away from those we like, we hope they will take the initiative to approach. By telling them "no", we expect they'll insist and struggle for the "yes". Nobody wears the mask of indifference to stay at a distance. On the contrary, we only keep the distance to give others more room to approach. That's our intention, and it is motivated in the unconscious belief that our feelings and thoughts are read by others, even with all our effort to keep them hidden. But misplaced beliefs like that are always mercilessly frustrated. When we wear the mask of indifference, people remain distant. If we remain distant, they don't approach. If we move away expecting they'll come to us, we remain alone. If we tell them "no", we also receive "no" as an answer. We forget that others also feel abandoned by our own indifference, and that they react to us as we do to them. We forget that they also keep away hoping we'll approach, and they tell us "no" expecting we'll insist and struggle for their "yes". Especially, we forget that they also unconsciously believe that their need for attention shines through the mask of indifference.

We maintain indifference and expect others to approach, and they keep theirs and expect we'll approach. The most common result of this equation is preserving the distance. In order to approach people who insist on keeping away, you need wit to understand the meaning of their distancing. Mostly, it takes detachment to let go of the resentment and the feeling of having been treated with indifference by them. For even when we understand the meaning of their distancing, pride sometimes plays a stronger role and makes us still keep our distance. Therefore, when there's no pride, one doesn't even need to understand anything. In the absence of pride and in the presence of affection, we seek those who are far without giving it much thought. But oh how these moments are rare! And oh how much better would the world be if they were more common!

97 – WE LIVE ALIENATED FROM SUFFERING

Many seek the psychologist wondering if there are any problems with them. They expect the psychologist to give them the answer. With easy access to information through the Internet, they research on psychiatric diagnosis and come to us fearing they have obsessive-compulsive, bipolar, or borderline disorder. It's as if a label could change their life. They imagine that the confirmation of the diagnosis by the psychologist will give them the certainty of having something wrong with them; and that the psychologist's denial would be the confirmation that everything is okay. This is more serious than it seems. We've lost the ability to know if there is something wrong with our lives. We need other people's opinion. As babies, if there was something wrong, we cried; if all was well, we were at peace. Our only criterion was suffering. If we suffered, something was wrong. If not, that meant all was well. As we get older, we seem to lose the ability to distinguish between being well or not. We only distinguish the "not being well" that is socially recognized as such. When we lose a loved one, when we end a relationship, lose our jobs, or suffer a severe physical or pathological condition, then we know we're not well. But if we enjoy full health, a good job, if we are in a steady relationship and have a prosperous life, we can't find socially acceptable reasons to be unwell. In this case, the un-wellness must have a medical justification. This is the main function of psychiatric diagnosis: providing a rationale to "not being well" when you can't find any other socially accepted justification. "How can she be unhappy? She's pretty, well employed, she's been in a steady relationship for so long, she has always been loved by her parents and have never experienced difficulties! Oh, is she borderline? That explains it"!

Only those who undergo physical and social difficulties, those victim of physical and psychological abuse, poverty or disease have the socially secured right to be unwell for life and make bad choices. Those who don't fit that profile need a medical excuse. The un-wellness of the poor is socially justified. The malaise of the middle and upper classes needs to be genetically and biochemically justified because there is no excuse for not being well. Therefore, when someone comes to the office wondering if they have any psychiatric problem, both the "yes" and the "no" are received with ambivalence. The "yes" means there is a problem, but it also means that from now on they have a reason for what they do and feel. The psychiatric diagnosis is socially accepted. And even though it might bother to carry the label initially, convenience ends up making the diagnosed cling to their diagnoses. The "no" on the other hand means that the patient is not ill, but it also means he won't be able to rely on labels, and there will be no socially accepted justification. The patient should engage then, through psychological and existential investigation, in the search for an

172

explanation that is still discredited by society. Thus, however great the relief of not being labeled by a diagnosis, it also brings, over time, a personal responsibility to solve the problem.

We don't understand suffering yet. In the absence of a background of illnesses, social problems, or serious recent events, we get lost. And because we don't understand suffering, we live as if we didn't suffer. I see the reluctance of some when they come for their session. Many only seek a psychologist when they can no longer lie to themselves and they force themselves to admit they're not well. Still, they are doubtful. They don't believe in their own suffering because no one takes them seriously. So if the psychologist refuses a psychiatric diagnosis but believes in their suffering, instant relief is produced. Suffering is no longer an experience for us; it is now an object of belief. Experiencing suffering is not enough to make us know that we're suffering. We need someone else to agree with us so that we allow ourselves to believe. Suffering no longer exists within us. Only doctors and intellectuals are able to locate it. For the rich, suffering ended up on the pages of diagnostic manuals; for the poor, it ended up in the pages of engaged sociology. Suffering became medical and political literature.

98 – "PANIC SYNDROME" AND OUR NEW WORLD OF UNCERTAINTIES

Until recently, life was full of certainties. We were raised to believe that once we grew up, we'd get married; once we graduated from college, we'd find good jobs; we would have children, and money, and after death came, we would find God and live happily forever in heaven. Those of us who are now 30 or 40 years old were the last generation raised with all these certainties and the first to come across the fact that they're no longer valid assurances. However, even those of past generations who got married and built their family and professional life as if obeying a screenplay are now forced to endure the anguish of seeing their remaining certainties fall, one after the other. Values and behavior change rapidly. All beliefs are under attack. Nothing is immune to the threat of change; nothing is safe anymore. In this scenario, we see psychiatric diagnoses multiply. People are using more and more drugs and less speech. We do not put anguish into words. Thus, it is difficult to resist the temptation of an industry and a socially recognized knowledge that insist on convincing us that our problems are biological and that medication is the solution.

To get on with life, we need some kind of support. Existence has always needed support. When we were children, family provided emotional and social security. In adolescence, social and romantic life awakened dreams and ideals within us that helped us handle conflicts and the anguish that was already strong. In adulthood, the occupation with work and children gave a sense of usefulness and accountability that kept us in a straight path. In old age, the comfort of religion was the source of the certainty that all would be well, and we would live happily ever after, after death, as in a fairy tale. Today, people become parents at a much older age and nonetheless remain unstable and adolescents in the way of being, which causes their children to experience adolescent conflicts while still in childhood. Teenagers feel no longer safe to experience. They are no longer sure they'll find their prince or princess one day. There are those who need to mark every relationship started with blood and a commitment ring as if it were their only and last chance to find someone, and there are those who, giving up the search for safety in relationships, only find it in the absence of involvement and promiscuity. Divorce and adultery haunt those who get married. How long will my lover want to be with me? Is my lover faithful to me? Shouldn't I also think about having a second lover? Shouldn't I also be prepared to have to leave him at any time? Children swiftly grow up and leave. The diploma that guarantees a job today doesn't guarantee anything tomorrow. The education that is sufficient today will be obsolete tomorrow. No job is a stable job, except for government jobs. It is better to earn less and have a stable, government job than to live in the uncertainty of the private sector. It is increasingly difficult to believe that life conducts itself by merit, that the best will be successful, the righteous will be rewarded, the wicked will be punished and the reckless will live in difficulty. Life seems indifferent to merit and actions, and that, more than all the scientific skepticism promoted by the media, has undermined the belief in the existence of an omnipotent being sensitive to our pain and effort, however great emphasis is made on denying any doubts or questions about it.

Many are collapsing. Crying spells for no apparent reason, a paralyzing terror that comes out of nowhere, the feeling of utter helplessness and impending death, the fear to take a simple step forward; as if it were no longer possible to keep breathing and stay in place. Not even the floor seems safe. Not even the floor seems stable. Suddenly, it's as if it could open and swallow us. The trivial way in which this "panic disorder" has been diagnosed isn't what is tragic; tragic is the inconclusive way it has been treated. There is no doubt that this new world of uncertainty requires a more reflective, less dogmatic and impulsive attitude. And there is no doubt that we are sinking deeper and deeper in thoughtlessness, impulsivity and blind dogmatism of easy solutions, be it a medical or religious dogmatism. More than ever before, we must think to live, and more than ever before, we are numbing our thinking capacity with drugs and dogmas. I cannot see an easy path ahead.

99 – THE ANTISOCIAL COUPLE

Nothing is more antisocial than a couple. A love relationship satisfies the need for stability and intimacy frustrated in social life. Whereas in social life no one belongs to anyone and intimacy is restricted by the limitations of physical contact, people in a love relationship belong to each other and take each other as their own without the constraints of social life. Also, while social life compels us to show the so-called formal maturity and kindness, that sense of humor and sobriety that buries our feelings and desires, in a love relationship we liberate our tantrums and our insecure, jealous, possessive and moody side. In this sense, the love relationship is antisocial by principle. And there's no problem with that. It's okay to seek in a relationship compensation for the

175

restrictions of our other relationships. If we find the satisfaction of our social life needs in our love relationship, its anti-sociability is benign. Problem arises when the couple's anti-sociability acquires a different meaning. When it replaces social life rather than compensating it, it becomes an inconvenience. If there are social life needs that only a romantic relationship can compensate, there are other needs only social life can satisfy. Social life also compensates needs not satisfied in the life as a couple. However, social life's diversity and instability has made the satisfaction of these needs difficult in a world of increasingly insecure people. Therefore, when people start life as a couple, it is a great temptation to seek in it not only compensation, but the replacement of social life.

At what point does life as a couple stops compensating for social life and starts to replace it? In the beginning of a life together, it is common to experience distancing from social life. There's no way to measure the distancing to determine to what extent it is good and where it becomes harmful. The most objective way of evaluating is to observe the conduct of the couple at social events. It's in social events that couples show the harmful sense of their anti-sociability. Two people that become a couple carry a background of a former social life. It is expected that with the start of a life together they share part of each other's social life. It is also likely that part of that social life will continue to demand the isolated presence of each one. The harmful sense of anti-sociability sense reveals itself in the difficulty of making this distinction. If, with the start of a life together, the previous social life of each becomes fully lived by both, something is wrong. For, unless both are socially skilled, the couple is more likely to isolate themselves in every event and continue relating only to each other. Thus, there is no actual social life. There's only the couple that continues to relate as a couple in a social event. This is frustrating for both the couple and for others. It is therefore natural that the couple start to avoid such events and restrict their social life only to events with other couples, the "double dates". Two couples that go out together to simulate the existence of a social life that has ceased to exist.

176

The harmful anti-social meaning of couple life is reflected in the increase of mutual dependence between the two. If life together becomes the couple's social life, they lose autonomy, including when it's time to end the relationship. How can one end a relationship that is someone's entire social life? What to do after the end? Who do they go to? How does one find another loving partner in a social life that became non-existent? More than a few people maintain relationships for longer than they should because they are frightened by these issues.

100 – AN EXPLANATION FOR BEHAVIOR AND THE PSYCHOLOGY OF EVERYDAY LIFE

Our philosophical and scientific theories provide explanations that relate causes to effects. Effect is not autonomous, but determined by the cause. In science, causal explanations showed their theoretical coherence and practical usefulness for the first time in Classical Physics. The determination principle in classical mechanics is mathematical. If two power units are applied on an object in direction A and one unit is applied in the same orientation but in the opposite direction B, the moving object will put itself on direction A with the force of one unit. It's as if the unit force applied in direction B didn't exist; as if the force applied in direction A were one rather than two units. Subtraction of opposing forces determines or causes the object's movement in direction A with the force of one unit. Proving its logical coherence, causalism and mathematical determinism prevailed in scientific explanations. It was inevitable that a scientific psychology was founded in the same paradigms. However, things don't work that way in Psychology.

We've all allowed ourselves to be frozen by fear. Who hasn't wanted to invite a friend out and feared receiving "no" as an answer? Who hasn't wanted to kiss someone and feared his reaction? Who never wanted to choose something dubious over something certain, for finding the dubious more seductive? However, although occasionally frozen, people invite each other out, take the risk of kissing without asking permission and choose dubious over certain. If we apply the same causal principle of classical mechanics, we should conclude that if the force of desire has prevailed over fear, then behavior was issued as if fear didn't exist. If there was, for example, two desire units in direction A and one fear unit in direction B, behavior went into motion by one unit of desire force in direction A. Thus, it's as if the unit of fear force applied in direction B didn't exist. And if fear didn't exist, it wasn't experienced.

We know things are not like that. We know that desire can overcome fear, but fear never lets itself be annulled. It is nonetheless experienced, and we can't even be sure that desire overcame fear. Sometimes it's not the force of desire that overcomes fear; it is fear itself that gets tired of fearing. In psychic dynamics, the forces do not cancel, subtract, or add each other up. They are experienced together, side by side. The equation of the psychic forces doesn't determine what we do, because this equation doesn't exist. A desire overcoming fear is a leap that crosses the infinite, as if the parable finally touched the axis X. If it were possible to quantify psychic forces, one force unit of fear could overcome one hundred force units of desire, because just by being there, no matter its strength, fear is a potential winner. The same goes for desire. And if it isn't the force of a desire or the force of a fear that determines the actions, reinforcing them can't determine them either.

Behavioral psychology explains behavior as the product of environmental factors that reinforce fears and desires. From this perspective, behavior is determined by the environment and has no autonomy. If this theory were true, the process of psychotherapy would consist of a mechanical procedure of reinforcing psychic forces and letting others fade into oblivion. However, even the psychologists working with this approach are forced to live with patients' resistance to their behavioral program. They explain their failures claiming it isn't possible to analyze all the environmental variables that determine behavior. There's the endless promise that research will make this analysis possible. And while they're not yet convinced of its impracticability, they ignore

178

the principle of indeterminacy in the explanation of behavior, that which we name subject or person. Subjectivity as a principle of indeterminacy forces us to admit that the explanation of behavior through environmental causes doesn't serve as a means of justification. This is the principle that makes us responsible for what we do. It also makes psychotherapy a critical process, not a method of causal remodeling of behavior. Even psychologists who advocate the deterministic nature of behavior make ethics and critical view the two pillars of psychotherapy. Psychotherapy is founded on criticism and ethics; clinical psychologists are formed in the ethics of positioning themselves critically in relation to their patients. If behavior were determined by the equation of environmental forces, neither criticism nor ethics would be necessary. It would be enough to alter those forces as we do in case of any body.

In order to change behavior, it isn't enough to just alter the environmental conditions surrounding the person. Even the strength of all the variables isn't enough to take from a person the awareness that his acts are products of their will. And the regret that sometimes succeeds our actions shows that the possibility of acting differently has always been there. To change the behavior, one must criticize it ethically. Nothing guarantees the change, but there's nothing else we can do. The psychology practiced by clinical psychologists is a psychology of ethics and criticism, regardless of its theoretical school. Within the four walls of a psychologist's office, behavior stops being object of scientific study and becomes the person, even in the relation with the most deterministic psychologists. When practiced, clinical psychology is no longer the theory that dehumanizes; it becomes knowledge about the ordinary life. By being practiced, clinical psychology becomes the psychology of everyday life.